Creating the
THOUGHTFUL
CLASSROOM

Strategies to Promote
Student Thinking

ANNE J. UDALL, Ph.D.
JOAN E. DANIELS, M.A.

ZEPHYR PRESS
Tucson, Arizona

Creating the Thoughtful Classroom:
Strategies to Promote Student Thinking

Grades 3–12

© 1991 Zephyr Press

ISBN: 0-913705-62-4

Editors: Emily DiSante, Stacey Lynn

Book Design and Production: Anne Olson, Casa Cold Type, Inc.

Zephyr Press
P.O. Box 66006
Tucson, Arizona 85728-6006

Contents

Acknowledgments

We always thought book acknowledgments were a bit excessive—listing numerous people and expressing gratitude to everyone you know. When we agreed to write this book, neither of us had any idea of the immensity of the undertaking. Now that the project is completed, we have a new understanding of acknowledgments. Truly, the parts of a book are far greater than the sum, and many people did help make a seemingly impossible task possible. It gives us great pleasure to acknowledge the support and guidance we have been offered along the way.

Our first priority is to thank the thinkers in the thinking field. So many bright, curious, and inquisitive individuals, past and present, have contributed freely their ideas and insights about thinking and the teaching of thinking. Theories and suggestions abound. A number of people in this field have greatly influenced our ideas and shaped many of our suggestions. We are grateful to Art Costa, David Perkins, Hilda Taba, Barbara Presseisen, Barry Beyer, Stanley Pogrow, and all the folks associated with the Association for Supervision and Curriculum Development (ASCD).

The people at Zephyr Press—Emily, Stacey, Jane, and Joey to name a few— were more than wonderful. Their feedback was invaluable, and all remained encouraging, steady, and straight-faced even when addressing our more ridiculous concerns.

A number of our colleagues/friends read the manuscript and made significant contributions. This book is a much stronger one as a result of all their efforts. First and foremost, we need to thank all the teachers in the "Creating the Thoughtful Classroom" project. All of us together were pioneers, breaking new ground. There was much laughter and sharing as we all learned how to be better teachers of thinking. Next, we gratefully thank Carolyn Landreth, Carol Cribbet-Bell, and Shirley Schiever. Both John Hosmer and Roger Shanley went beyond the call of duty or friendship.

Our families and friends were the final part of the support system that surrounded us during this process. Anne would like to thank a number of people: Darcy, Adam, Barbara, Phyllis, Bonnie, Carol, and Ed. Joan also acknowledges the tremendous support of her family. Co-authoring a book, like teaching in the classroom, forces other things to the back burner. All too often it was family. Libby picked up the little ones at day care. Rhoda endured much complaining about self-inflicted injuries. At work, Norma was a great team teacher and friend.

As for mutual acknowledgments, which we assume everyone expects: next to getting married or becoming cellmates, co-authoring a book is the best means for really getting to know someone. We are still friends.

Introduction

The idea that teachers need to teach students how to think on complex levels is not a new one for either of us. Anne has worked with gifted students for over ten years, and Joan has been an innovative, challenging regular classroom teacher for over fifteen years. We have worked together on a number of complex-level units for students and recently have been part of a project to increase the teaching of complex-level thinking in the regular classroom. Writing a book about our experiences of teaching complex-level thinking had been percolating in Anne's head for awhile, and when the people at Zephyr Press called, the ideas now had a place to bloom. This book is the culmination of over two years of hard work.

As we began to write, it became increasingly clear that changing the "status quo" of the classroom was a monumental task, and such a transformation does not occur overnight. Time and effort were needed. Results were inevitable but often indiscernible at first. In fact, creating the thoughtful classroom was akin to taking a journey, with teachers as the tour guides.

So, our book is about this journey of change from one style to another style of teaching. We have based the content of this book on current thinking in the field, but more important, we have grounded it in our personal experiences in the classroom. We have tried every suggestion in the book—in fact, if an idea is here, we have used it successfully.

The first three chapters of the book focus on broad ideas concerning thinking and teaching of complex-level thinking. If the thinking skills movement is new to you, we highly recommend reading the early chapters first. In chapters 4 through 7, we focus on the pragmatic realities of teaching thinking in the regular classroom, first discussing the thinking lesson in detail. The heart of the book is contained in chapters 6 and 7, in which we explain the roles of teacher and students in the evolution of the thoughtful classroom. In the last chapter, we discuss how to evaluate progress on the journey.

Some of us are further along the path than others on the journey to teach thinking. The book follows a chronological outline, starting at the beginning of the trip with a description of the various preparations one must make and exploring the stops along the way. We invite you to seek out the parts of the book most applicable to your level of awareness and interest. We hope that you find the challenge of creating the thoughtful classroom as exhilarating as we both do. Bon voyage!

1

Creating the Thoughtful Classroom: Taking the Ultimate Journey

My idea of education is to unsettle the minds of the young, and to inflame their intellects.

Robert Hutchins

The HOT topic in education today is complex-level thinking—what it is and how to teach it. Evidence of this concern abounds in universities, schools, homes, and businesses. In the academic hallways, eminent philosophers in education argue over the true nature of thinking. Scholars separate the components of complex-level thinking into various categories, the result of which is a bewildering array of available models and confusing terminology. Theories are everywhere. School boards and superintendents insist that complex thinking be part of the school curriculum. Parents and business leaders worry about the inability of students to think in a sophisticated manner. National reports call for more complex thinking from our students.[1]

This intense focus on thinking has been fairly recent. In the 1970s and 1980s, American society placed little value on provocative dialogue; and, as schools mirror the political and economic structure of the society they serve, they consequently did not specifically teach thinking. More emphasis was placed on mastering basic skills than on mastering skillful thinking. Now, however, the emphasis has shifted toward teaching critical thinking. When asked, business and political leaders clearly state that future graduates need to be able to think critically, solve problems, and be creative.[2] Today teachers are being asked to teach students how to think with sophistication and complexity.

In response, teachers in our nation's classrooms struggle to incorporate thinking lessons into their already full day. The actual *teaching* of thinking confronts the practitioner with an age-old dilemma: "Yes, that's fine, but how do I do that in *my* classroom?" Because of lack of time or support, many teachers answer this question by occasionally assigning a "complex-thinking worksheet" or conducting a "thought-provoking" discussion with their students. Yet, although complex thinking is supposedly occurring, it is sporadic and undirected at best. A classroom of thinkers can be created only through systematic reflection and planning.

This is a book about how to create what we call the "thoughtful classroom," where teachers and students value thinking and engage in thoughtful discourse on a regular basis.[3] We use the metaphor of two possible journeys to describe the difference between the classroom where thinking occurs sporadically and the thoughtful classroom, where thinking is systematically integrated. As teachers, we take a journey with our students each year. The trip lasts nine months, but the destinations and sights along the way vary dramatically depending on our values and training. We are the tour guides; we select the route.

Two journeys are available for most teachers.

Two journeys are available for most teachers. Package A, "The See-It-All-Plan," takes you everywhere, on a whirlwind tour. The tour guide directs and orchestrates your every move. The itinerary is rigid and very full. You cover incredible amounts of territory. You touch down on every continent, see every statue, visit every museum, shop every tourist trap, sample every cuisine, hear every language—in short, do it all!

Package B, "The Immersion Plan," moves much slower. The tour guide has a specific origin and destination and has selected interim sites carefully. However, opportunities abound for spontaneous and independent sightseeing. During this journey, you are required to disembark the tour bus and take "in-depth" side trips. You ask the locals how, why, and where questions. You are encouraged to interact with the tour guide and your traveling companions. The tour guide facilitates discussions that compare, contrast, and analyze what is being seen. Travelers on this tour often comment that they have enjoyed themselves so much that they are planning another trip—this time without the tour guide.

The first journey, Package A, describes the route for the teacher who is more interested in quantity than quality. This teacher's classroom is characterized by an intense focus on the prescribed curriculum, isolated bits of content, and teacher-directed activities. Thinking occurs either by accident or because the textbook contains a few isolated thinking exercises.

In contrast, Package B describes the journey toward creation of the thoughtful classroom. This classroom will appear in a wide variety of forms, some indistinguishable at first glance, but all characterized by curious, eager, and open exchanges among the participants. Teachers will be facilitators, not authorities, of knowledge; students will become self-motivated, disciplined thinkers.

Many teachers are eager to take the second journey. Such a trip is a more rigorous one, but a thoughtful classroom is one of the most exciting places to be in education today. This book is about how to create such a place—the concerns of the tour guide, the various maps you can find, luggage requirements, and the actual activities undertaken on the nine-month journey.

Why One More Book about Thinking?

Our commitment to writing this book grew out of our participation in a project to help teachers teach thinking better. The project, called Creating the Thoughtful Classroom (CTC), involved ten to fifteen teachers. In the first year, students worked with a thinking-skills specialist in a pullout program. A thinking-skills curriculum was designed; in addition, teachers identified a number of important teacher strategies that encourage complex-level thinking. The regular classroom teacher came to the resource program with the students and observed the specialist teaching complex-level thinking lessons. Teachers were then expected to practice the teaching of thinking in their own classrooms.

In the second year of the project, some major changes were made. For example, a peer coaching model was initiated. Instead of the specialist teaching, the classroom teacher taught weekly thinking lessons as part of the regular curriculum and was coached by the thinking-skills specialist. The weekly lessons were focused on developing the thinking-skills curriculum and specific teacher strategies. In addition, regular classroom teachers coached each other and met regularly to share ideas, research, and evaluation.

The success of this project depended largely on the teacher, who was responsible for planning and teaching the lesson. We found, from the outset, that the behavior of the teacher was the key to success—more important than the thinking processes we selected to develop or the lessons we planned. The teacher set the tone and the direction; without specific teacher strategies and dispositions, any efforts to create the thoughtful classroom were doomed.

In our quest to learn more about the role of the teacher in teaching thinking, we reviewed much of the available material. We located various models of teaching thinking, lists of thinking skills and processes, and worksheets and workbooks to teach specific thinking skills and processes.

Although many of these books were invaluable, we did not find the book we needed: a book dedicated solely to developing the thoughtful classroom, with the main focus on the roles of the teacher *and* the students. This book we couldn't find would be pragmatic but well researched, written by teachers for teachers. The realities and limitations of the regular classroom would be understood by the authors of this book. Special training in a specific model or knowledge of a particular theory would not be required for an understanding of the book's contents; instead, the suggestions in the book would be applicable to any curriculum being used. This book would give teachers a simple overview of the thinking field for orientation but would not advocate any one program. It would, rather, clearly define strategies and behaviors of the teacher and students in the thoughtful classroom. Ideas for integrating the teaching of thinking into the classroom curriculum would be suggested. Finally, this book would give some simple, manageable ideas on how to evaluate teacher strategies and student behavior in the thoughtful classroom.

But such a book was nowhere to be found—so we set out to write it.* What we wanted was a collection of ideas for individuals, in all areas of education, who want to enhance their teaching of complex-level thinking by focusing on teacher strategies and student behaviors. Some of our readers may already be using a district- or school-adopted complex-level thinking curriculum; others may simply be incorporating thinking into their individual classrooms or be considering such a change. Regardless of your status, this book will help you become a better teacher of thinking.

---

*Lest we sound arrogant or unfamiliar with already available materials: we know that much of the information contained within these pages has been reported in other sources and places. We are grateful to the many authors who are pioneering ideas and techniques in this field, and we list the most significant influences on our work in appendixes A and B.

What Have We Learned about Teaching Thinking?

The tone and focus of this book have been formed by our combined twenty-six years of involvement in gifted education, regular classrooms, academia, and most recently, the above-mentioned thinking project. In this section, we would like to share with you some of the insights we have gained about creating a thoughtful classroom.

When we first started teaching thinking, we found it was a hard, sometimes frustrating challenge. We were faced with familiar, comfortable patterns of behavior in ourselves and our students that were difficult to change. At the beginning, it was easy to give up or at least to ask what was going wrong. "Is it us or is it the students?" we wondered.

Yet, because both teacher and students play a role in the classroom dynamic, the responsibility must lie with both partners. Our part was obvious. We "invited" our students to have discussions, to think with us, by asking *why*—yet once we received an answer to why, we seldom had the know-how to develop the lesson further. We might have asked a few questions, even had some interesting exchanges, but eventually a dead-end was reached. Our university training did not prepare us to teach students to think, and we lacked role models—our colleagues took the same teacher training courses we did.

Students tend to be passive learners, travelers who have long ago learned to sit still and watch the scenery pass. When we asked them to think, they struggled. Television and life have taught them quick comebacks, flip responses, and pat answers—but few reflective abilities. Children have learned not to listen to each other or to their teachers. This is not to say our students don't know how or don't want to think. They do, but they have not been taught; students have had little practice and even less guidance.

When our project first started, many of the teachers believed they were already teaching thinking. Most were—when a particular lesson demanded some reasoning. Yet, creating a thoughtful classroom goes beyond the occasional "current events" discussion or science experiment. To change habitual behaviors, new ones must be practiced on a continual and systematic basis. The most important lesson we learned, therefore, was that if these familiar roles were to be changed and a classroom of thinkers created in its place, teachers must establish a conscious goal to do so.

Having set this goal, we then learned that constructing the thoughtful classroom required four crucial ingredients:

- time;
- the commitment to try new ideas;
- the belief that thinking on complex levels is an essential goal for students; and
- the conviction that all students are capable of thinking on complex levels.

Without these four components, the venture would fail.

The last lesson we learned was that once you set the goal of building the thoughtful classroom, the dynamics of the classroom change forever. Change always involves the unknown and can be scary. At first, you might feel awkward and strained; your students may seem startled or unresponsive to your new attempts. But, as you learn new strategies and behaviors, your students do too. With time, you will no longer be the authority with all the "right answers," and your students will cease to be passive learners.

A classroom of thinkers is incompatible with a controlled, rigid setting. If you are committed to creating a thoughtful classroom, you must be ready to accept more active, questioning, curious students. This does not require a forfeiture of discipline or time on task. Instead, the thinking classroom moves toward inner discipline and demands greater focus on task. Though it may take greater intellectual energy on your part, such a classroom can be an invigorating, energizing, and challenging place to be!

What This Book Is and What This Book Is Not

This book will help you cultivate your ability to initiate a thinking dialogue among thirty children. The statements below more specifically tell you what this book is and what it is not; these are our guarantees to you.

What This Book Is

This book

- is practical, easy to read, and easy to digest. It is based on personal experience as well as current research/ information in the field. The ideas in this book are both original and borrowed (but properly referenced).

- is by and for both elementary and secondary teachers of all types of students. The degree of intelligence of the learner does not drive the teaching of complex-level thinking. We truly believe that all students can think and that the process of thinking can be learned and improved upon. Children of all ages and learning styles can benefit from the techniques we suggest.

- will identify some of the common concerns teachers have about teaching thinking, such as "Where will I ever find the time to do *one* more thing?" (chapter 2).

- will provide you with a concise overview of the major thinking skills and models. We identify both similarities and differences (chapter 3).

- will discuss the necessary classroom environment for fostering complex thinking and suggest a framework for the planning and teaching of complex-thinking lessons (chapter 4).

- will give you a number of ideas about how to integrate complex-level thinking into your classroom content in the areas of language arts, social studies, math, and science. Ways of using textbooks, nontextbooks, and different types of media are shared (chapter 5).

- will identify teacher strategies and student behaviors that, when displayed, will increase the amount of thinking done in your class by both you and your students. We will give you and your students specific hints to increase competence in each strategy and behavior and discuss the relationship between teacher strategies and student behaviors (chapters 6 and 7).

- will tell you different ways to assess whether you are increasing the thoughtful student and teacher behaviors that initiate and encourage complex-level thinking in your classroom (chapter 8).

What This Book Is Not

This book

This book will not . . .

- will not give you a static model (with all the parts and glue prepackaged) for teaching thinking in your classroom.

- will not provide you with packaged activities to use with students. In other words, this is not a recipe book. You will have to extrapolate from the ideas and hints we provide. We have confidence that you will prefer to add your own content and style.

- is not a repair manual. It assumes good teaching is in place already. The thoughtful classroom is built upon a solid foundation. If the foundation needs to be built this year, start teaching thinking skills next year.

Who You Are and Who You Are Not

All teachers can be taught to be better teachers of thinking. We have written this book to benefit all teachers who want to improve the amount of thinking their students do. However, our experience has taught us that certain teachers are more likely than others to be successful at teaching thinking. This is not to say you are *good* if you can teach thinking and *bad* if you cannot. Schools are full of people with different skills and values; that is as it should be. Some of us are really good at teaching basic skills; others excel at teaching reading; some have the touch with special education students.

So, who is likely to be most successful at teaching thinking? Here's a profile. You are a classroom teacher. You have a graduate degree or are considering obtaining one. You are committed to education as a profession and are interested in new ideas or topics in the field. You are willing to devote a reasonable but not excessive amount of time to other tasks in your classroom besides grading papers. You are frustrated by the lack of practical, classroom-based materials for the teaching of thinking. You are aware that tomorrow's world will be different from today's, that we are becoming a more complex, intertwined "planet Earth." You believe that because of vast changes in the world, students will need the ability to think concisely, with sophistication and depth. Most of all, you value thinking not only in your classroom but also in other areas of your life.

Indeed, we are convinced that in order to teach thinking, we must value thinking in our own lives. As we all know, actions speak louder than words. So for those of you who are still interested, we have provided a checklist of behaviors exhibited by people who value thinking. This test is a quick, nonscientific, tongue-in-cheek way for you to determine how much you value thinking in your life. If you don't (a) answer yes to many of the questions, (b) relate to any of the statements, or (c) think the survey is funny, save this book for awhile and then read it again. However, if you do answer yes and/or laugh as you read, you are probably going to enjoy this book.

Do You Value Thinking?
Teacher Test

This test is based on the metacognitive exploration of respected educators currently practicing in the field of thinking instruction. The characteristics were standardized against a population of veteran educators for validity and predictability. A significantly higher number of yes answers will predict that the candidate currently engages in thinking-type lessons in the classroom or will most likely do so in the near future.

	YES	NO
1. Do you drift off at faculty meetings?	❑	❑
2. Do you make a personal contract to resign if you have to attend one more presentation for recruitment of band and orchestra students?	❑	❑
3. Do you tend to drift off into those old What is the meaning of life? reveries while doing the fourth load of laundry?	❑	❑
4. Do you have a tendency to jump passionately into projects, staying up till midnight, forgetting that nothing may come of all the energy?	❑	❑
5. Do you become frustrated with the routine side of teaching and all the paperwork?	❑	❑
6. Do you still get a charge out of controversial discussions with students, friends, and family?	❑	❑
7. Do you read books? (Hiding in the bathroom to do so counts.)	❑	❑
8. Do you value quiet opportunities to think? (Hiding in the bathroom counts here too.)	❑	❑
9. Do you understand Gary Larson cartoons, Doonesbury, and in the past, *Harvard Lampoon, Mad Magazine,* or similar ilk?	❑	❑
10. Do you wish you understood *A Short History of Time*?	❑	❑
11. Do you every once in awhile take (or yearn to take) a risk—rappelling, parachuting, driving in California, giving a speech, taking a class in some other area besides education?	❑	❑
12. Do you feel comfortable with disagreement in discussions? (This doesn't necessarily mean you are disagreeable.)	❑	❑
13. Do you get (or did you **used** to get) in trouble for asking questions?	❑	❑
14. Do you appreciate the creative, if troublesome, kid in your class?	❑	❑
15. Do you find that some people label you "troublesome"?	❑	❑
16. Do you find that some people label you "persistent"?	❑	❑
17. Do you wake up having solved a problem you toiled over the day before?	❑	❑
18. Do you relish the opportunity to play word games with people?	❑	❑
19. Do you see the world as full of exciting opportunities?	❑	❑
20. Do you yearn for more hours in the day?	❑	❑

TOTAL YES = _____

Score	Prediction for Your Students
20-16 Yes	Students in this person's classroom will have the ride of their lives.
15-11 Yes	Students in this person's classroom will stay on their toes.
10-6 Yes	Students in this person's classroom will perform well on standardized tests.
5-0 Yes	Students in this person's classroom will need to know resuscitation techniques.

Conclusion

Every journey begins with a single step. The suggestions in this book, taken in small steps, will help you be a better teacher of complex-level thinking. No single book can give you the full range of skills, and this one is no exception. Time and commitment are necessary. Perhaps you have begun to learn about the teaching of thinking because your school district demands it or you have a vague, nagging feeling that your students don't think enough. Your level of enthusiasm may range from lukewarm to energized and ready to go. Regardless of your original motives, as you begin to create a thoughtful classroom and notice the changes in your students (and yourself!), your thinking lessons will become some of the most stimulating and challenging educating you do in your classroom. You will find that being a tour guide can be an exhilarating profession.

Every journey begins with a single step.

2

Teaching Thinking:
The Concerns of the Tour Guide

If we would have new knowledge, we must get a
whole world of new questions.

Susan Langer

Before embarking on a journey, a tour guide has many responsibilities—scheduling the trip, sequencing events, determining content of lectures, and satisfying clients. Like a tour guide, the teacher has many similar concerns when embarking on the goal of achieving a thoughtful classroom. All of us on this journey face some persistent questions and dilemmas that become apparent upon our departure. We will focus on these issues in this chapter.

First and foremost is the problem of time. How long will it take to do the job well? On what part of the process do we linger the longest? Can we find the time we need?

Second, how do we successfully teach both content and process, and how do we balance the amount of each? Do we want children to learn to take trips independently or do we want them to learn the "content" of a particular trip? In fact, can they learn both? Do we want to impart a background of experiences, such as the history, culture, and magnificence of Rome, for example—or do we want to spend the extra time teaching about the causes and effects of the inevitable collapse of that culture?

Third, should all students have lessons in thinking skills?

Fourth, how do we structure such a trip? What vehicles do we use? How do we arrange the travelers—in small groups, large groups, or one on one?

11

Fifth, how do we convince others, such as parents and principals, that the trip is worth the price?

And, last, how do we get others to join us? A lot can be learned from colleagues, some of whom have been there before and have valuable resources to share.

Such questions beg for answers. Like so many issues in education, it is easier to identify and discuss the problems than it is to pinpoint solutions. No one has quick or easy resolutions to any of the questions we raise here; however, awareness of both the questions and the lack of easy solutions will make us better teachers of thinking. Some say nothing short of a radical restructuring of our schools will allow in-depth teaching of complex thinking in the classroom.[1] For most of us, however, the revolution is not coming quickly, and we must work within the pragmatic realities of today's schools. Because of these realities, we are forced to accept incomplete answers to some of these questions and invent creative solutions to others. When addressing these concerns in the next sections, we will offer both the incomplete and the creative solutions we have discovered.

How Much Time Will I Need When I Have So Little Already?

Teachers mistakenly assume that they can simply incorporate thinking discussions into the curriculum without stealing time from other areas. Teachers who first hear about teaching thinking skills commonly respond: "I teach thinking all the time—this will be no different." On the surface, this statement is true for many teachers. We suggest, however, upon closer examination that most teachers teach thinking as an afterthought, using questions at the end of the chapter for extra credit or incorporating an isolated worksheet or two during the week. Yet, to teach thinking well requires both a conscious effort *and* time.

Time is a formidable issue with teachers who attempt to switch from the traditional curriculum to one that elicits thinking skills. The "time problem" has two parts: preparation and teaching.

Teachers need lots of preparation time to teach thinking properly. (We will outline, in other chapters, the specifics of planning a thinking lesson.) We have found that, at least initially, preparation time is nearly as long as teaching time. Naturally, finding this time is difficult when a teacher has only twenty percent of the day for planning. In addition, preparation is more often in the form of active thinking about the lesson—intellectualizing, pondering, and questioning the material to be presented—rather than the relatively simple task of gathering materials or reproducing worksheets. In short, planning for a thinking lesson takes creativity and focused reflection. It can seldom be accomplished while monitoring after-school study hall.

Even if a teacher takes "after hours" time for planning, the second issue arises. A thinking lesson needs time, regardless of your content. Students need a "warm-up" period, an active thinking period, and then the chance to "cool down." To teach complex thinking in less than an hour is difficult if not impossible. With the school day already full of curriculum requirements, where will this time come from?

Curriculum guides for most school districts neatly divide the teaching day into compartments of time that must be spent on specific areas of the curriculum. Most teachers feel duty bound to teach specific basic skills during a student's annual tenure. Take the typical sixth-grade teacher: "I really expect my kids to add, subtract, divide, and multiply fractions by the time they leave my class." Or the English teacher across the hall: "Don't send them on to me without making sure they can write a complete sentence." The junior-high-school staff says: "If you send them knowing the metric system and keyboarding, we'll do the rest." "We can't discuss the classics when reading skills are so poor," say the teachers at the high school.

Concrete skills like these are more easily, if not accurately, measured and are the criteria by which school districts and communities measure success. Drop the concept of thinking skills into this concrete, compartmentalized, measurable world, and many people become nervous. Although thinking skills are inherent in even the worst curriculums, they don't quite fit into any category. Therefore, the teacher who wants to teach thinking is left with the problem of finding time to teach thinking *and* everything else!

We do not demean the necessity of teaching basic skills. We believe they are just that—basic. We cannot be capricious about our role to teach children the basic skills necessary to survive in a literate society. However, the school day has a limited number of hours. Like sugar that is dissolved in water, thinking skills can be absorbed within the curriculum to a point. Consider this old science experiment:

The teacher puts a brim-full glass of water on the table. She then holds up a metal cube. What will happen when the cube is dropped in the liquid? The water will overflow. Tablespoons of sugar are shown to the students and predictions requested. Will it overflow? Sugar is added—tablespoons, in fact—yet no overflow occurs. Sugar can become incorporated between the molecules of water—it dissolves into the tiny spaces. Eventually, however, at saturation, the water will overflow.

Eventually the teaching of thinking skills will demand its own space (i.e., when the curriculum reaches saturation), and other parts of the curriculum will be eliminated or assimilated.

Opportunity Cost

The increasing pressure to teach complex thinking in our classrooms requires some difficult choices for administrators and theorists. Until now, it has been easier to avoid the decisions than to face them. But educational leaders must acknowledge from the outset that thinking strategies will displace other subjects in the curriculum. Lauren Resnick, a well-respected educational psychologist, calls it "opportunity cost." Recognizing the time constraints that classroom teachers face each day, Resnick insists, nevertheless, that we must be willing to "give up" or consolidate parts of the established curriculum to include more thinking skills.[2]

In summary, fully incorporating thinking into our curriculums will occur only when we drastically change our notions of what should be taught in our schools. Some educators have started to advocate new concepts of curriculum,[3] but we are a long way from integrating these new ideas into our daily teaching routines. Until time is consciously planned for the teaching of thinking, we must look at our individual curriculums and consolidate, give up, or judiciously "dissolve" thinking processes into content teaching. But how?

Content and Thinking Processes:
How Do I Successfully Teach Both?

A ninth-grade class spent nine weeks in social studies studying the concept of culture. First, students categorized culture into subclasses: government, religion, economics, family, and so on. Then, they discovered common traits in their own cultures and subsequently in their teen subcultures. They viewed tapes of both nontechnological (e.g., tribes in Africa) and contemporary cultures (e.g., western European countries), looking for examples of the cultural categories and analyzing their significance. The students looked for relationships between geography and culture. They were given certain geographical conditions and were asked to predict cultures that would arise from these conditions (e.g., what kind of culture might evolve on a tropical island?). Finally, they created their own cultures, complete with artifacts and a language.

That same nine weeks could have been spent learning facts about ancient Greek or European cultures. Certain administrators may rightfully ask how the teacher could justify the time spent on something so "content free" (the unit didn't stress facts and figures). The material, however, was hardly content free; it simply *appeared* that way because the teacher spent considerable time expanding the understanding of key concepts—*culture* and *cultural categories*—and then used those concepts to compare, predict, and analyze. The unit established a framework upon which other studies of specific cultures could take place.

This example illustrates how teachers interested in teaching complex thinking struggle with the question of how to teach both classroom content and complex thinking successfully. The options available to teachers range on a continuum: on one end, teachers teach thinking processes as a separate course; at the other end, teachers integrate the teaching of thinking into the regular curriculum. Along the continuum are a number of other choices, including a combination of the two approaches just outlined.

Robert Ennis uses the term *general method* to describe the teaching of thinking as a separate course and the term *immersion method* to describe the other end of the continuum.[4] A teacher uses the general method (sometimes called *direct teaching*) when he or she teaches thinking separately from the regular class curriculum. The thinking skill is named and then taught directly. For example, time might be set aside weekly for a thinking lesson. One week, students are introduced to "inferring skills." These skills are defined and identified, and students have an opportunity to practice them. Difficult or confusing content is kept at a minimum so as not to interfere with the learning of the skill. This example, although simplistic, gives a quick overview of the general approach. Workbook materials that propose to teach complex thinking often use the direct teaching method.

In contrast, a teacher uses the immersion method when he or she teaches thinking skills as part of a regular classroom lesson. The content of the lesson will be part of the curriculum. For example, students might study the Civil War and use inference skills during the lesson. They learn facts and then draw inferences from them. The main characteristics of each approach are summarized in the following chart:

Methods of Teaching Thinking

General Method	*Immersion Method*
• Thinking is taught as a separate skill.	• Thinking is taught as part of the regular classroom lessons.
• Skill or process is identified for students.	• Skill or process is not identified for students.
• Content is unrelated to classroom curriculum.	• Content is part of regular curriculum.
• Content is kept simple, so as not to interfere with the teaching of the thinking process.	• The teacher is usually responsible for the design of the lesson.
• Many commercial programs use this approach.	• Some commercial programs use this approach.[5]

Between these two ends of the continuum lies the *conceptual-infusion approach.*[6] This approach restructures standard curriculum content in such a way as to teach both good thinking and content (knowledge). The major difference between the infusion and immersion methods is that, in the former, the thinking skill is made explicit. Using the previous example concerning the Civil War, the teacher would say: "Today the thinking skill we are going to use when talking about the Civil War is making inferences."

The earlier example of the cultural unit illustrates the conceptual-infusion approach. The concept of culture was taught in concert with the teaching of thinking skills. Students learned content conceptually while engaging in complex thinking. In fact, when teaching content this way, complex thinking is the natural outcome.

We prefer the conceptual-infusion approach, for both pragmatic and theoretical reasons. First, the infused method is definitely the best way to use limited time. Second, identifying the skill directly for students increases awareness and metacognitive ability (to be discussed in the next chapter). Finally, until research is more definitive as to which approach is the best, we like the one that combines the best of all methods. We propose that, like sugar in water, the teaching of thinking skills can be incorporated into your curriculum. Some content will be sacrificed or selectively abandoned,[7] but we maintain that the ability to think is at least as important as memorizing selected facts.

Which Students Should Get the Thinking Skills?

It is not hard to accept that gifted students need the extra challenge of complex-thinking exercises. For such students, teachers can easily justify stealing from the required content areas. Most of us still feel okay about teaching thinking to our average and below-average students *if* we teach the regular curriculum too. Yet a major dilemma arises when we consider the other students in our classrooms. What about students who spend much of their time struggling to complete assignments? Or students with limited backgrounds or experience? Can they learn to question, evaluate, and make decisions? Will they benefit from complex-thinking lessons? Remember, critics often worry about how ignorant our students are in areas like math and geography. Aren't we doing such students a disfavor?

Our underlying belief is that all students can and should learn to think better. Different students will produce different levels of thinking. You may need to wait longer for some students and perhaps push them harder, but it has been our experience that with practice all students in the regular classroom can think. Many do as well as or better than their "brighter" peers when the class structure demands their active participation. The rewards from teaching students to think on complex levels greatly outweigh any loss of basic skills or regular content. The choice is between passive observers for whom each problem is new and active learners who attack each problem with a set of skills that breed confidence and success.

How Will the Classroom Look Different?

Thoughtful classrooms look different from traditional classrooms. In traditional classrooms, the teacher does most of the talking, conveying information from a position of authority and control. In thinking classrooms, the teacher facilitates and encourages students to challenge, ponder, and take risks. Students frequently disagree with each other and with the teacher.

Activities in the thoughtful classroom range from large-group, teacher-directed discussions to cooperative learning groups. Teachers who present concepts in a whole-group, teacher-directed arena as well as those who favor small-group, cooperative learning activities can have their needs met in this type of classroom.

Students with different learning styles can also have their needs met. People often associate the teaching of thinking with highly verbal activities and worry that students who do not talk frequently or coherently may lose the opportunity to be challenged. Yet thinking can be done through both discussion and active learning activities, so the learning styles of all students can be accommodated.

In the discussion format, teachers and students engage in discussion as the primary means of communicating ideas and thoughts. Social studies and language arts activities lend themselves to this structure. Although many people associate discussions with large groups only, dialogue can also occur in small groups, with teachers and/or students leading.

In the active-learning format, students and teacher engage in thinking tasks that involve manipulatives and/or hands-on activities. For example, teachers would use this format when asking students to design a science experiment or build a model to scale.

The key to teaching thinking is knowing when to use what type of structure. The two types of formats can occur in total or small groupings, as follows:

+ Total group—teacher directed
+ Total group—student directed
+ Small group—cooperative learning

No format is the "right" way to teach thinking. One cannot identify a thoughtful classroom by the way the desks are arranged at any one time. We have found that the needs of the learning group as well as the particular skills and content determine the structure of the classroom. A mature, task-oriented group can move quite swiftly from a teacher-directed to a student-directed format and finally into small groups engaged in cooperative learning. The groups return to a teacher-directed, whole-group format when the content or process requires new direction. The key is in selective variation.

As the thoughtful classroom slowly takes form, the dynamics between teacher and students will change. Such change can be scary and, at times, unnerving. On the other hand, the new interactions can be stimulating and exciting! Students become active, curious learners, no longer willing to accept the teacher as the sole authority. They question the teacher and each other. They argue and debate. A level of energy and excitement exists that was not there before. The thoughtful classroom holds constant surprise.

How Do We Get Principals, Parents, and Other Taxpayers to Support the Trip?

Perhaps much of the job of convincing the public to finance such a trip has already been done. In chapter 1, we briefly mentioned the strong demands from business, political, and educational leaders to teach our children how to think and reason. Our problem, then, is not to convince the public that thinking needs to be taught, but to decide *how* to do it.

Change can occur on an individual and on a national scale. We can begin the process of change by becoming advocates for the teaching of complex thinking in our schools. Inform parents with notes and letters about what you are doing in your classroom. Talk to your colleagues and involve them in planning and teaching. Make sure your principal is aware of the necessity for thinking skills (hand her or him a copy of this book!). Have the teaching of thinking be a conscious, overt goal at your school.

On a national scale, strong leadership from educators dedicated to the teaching of thinking skills will be necessary for change. Unfortunately, it's difficult right now to find a group of educators who have one mind about what schools should be teaching. However, national organizations such as the Association for Supervision and Curriculum Development (ASCD) and the National Council of Teachers of Mathematics (NCTM) are at the forefront of the thinking-skills movement. Not only are these groups insisting on change, but they are also making concrete suggestions on how that change might look.

How Do We Find Others on the Same Journey?

Among the rank and file are many teachers who have developed a style that encourages the emergence of the thoughtful classroom. However, few have had the opportunity to refine and label what they do, and almost no one has had the time to talk to others. We don't think such teachers will be hard to find.

Teachers must gather to discuss the thoughtful classroom. Teachers need on-the-job time (not necessarily money) and the opportunity to maximize collegiality. A thinking curriculum is neither a set of books nor some boxes of manipulatives on the shelves. It is, first and foremost, an approach to teaching. No text adoption can do it; no set of kits will force it. Only intelligent discourse with other educators will lead to teams of teachers who conduct thinking curriculums. You can begin looking for other teachers by talking to your peers, subscribing to national journals and magazines on this topic, and attending local and national conferences.

Conclusion

It is clear that the difficult issues of time, the appropriate balance of content and process, classroom structure, and professional support are formidable obstacles. Yet we believe that you *can* teach thinking, even with such pressing concerns. In the following chapters we will give you numerous ideas on how to develop the thoughtful classroom. The most important ingredient is your willingness to try some new things. See how you solve the problems of time, curriculum focus, and parental support in your own classroom. Your solutions may be similar to the ones we have proposed here, or perhaps you will find different, equally successful answers. However, before embarking on our trip, let's have a look at what other people have said about thinking and the teaching of thinking.

3

Quiet in the Back Seat:
Just Pass Me the Map

Will the real thinking please stand up?

Ron Brandt and David Perkins

Let's imagine that you have bought your ticket for the journey and you know your destination is the thoughtful classroom. Locating the right map is next; you need to know the best routes and places for in-depth investigation. Your best friend tells you about the *Many T's* ("Thinkers Who Think about Thinking and Try to Tell Teachers How to Teach It") catalogue, where it is possible to purchase maps.

Excitedly, you locate a catalogue and thumb through. The selection is overwhelming; you never knew so many maps were available. As you read the description of each map, the realization dawns quickly: no two maps are the same nor is any map easy to read. "We have to stop here. . . . It's shorter this way. . . . We don't have time to go that way. . . . It's better to head west than east."

You never knew so many maps were available.

You put the catalogue down, bewildered and confused. Clearly, no single diagram exists. In fact, locations and distances seem subjective. The catalogue even warns that maps and scales are being erased and drawn continually.

How, then, does one achieve the destination of the thoughtful classroom with such a large selection of possible routes? Learning what all the maps have in common is an important first step. Although a bewildering number of models are available on thinking and on teaching thinking, it is not our intent to describe and critique them.

20

We endeavor to provide you with an overview so that you can begin to find your way through the confusing maze of terminology and ideas on teaching thinking. This chapter will give you

- a basic idea of what the term "thinking" means,

- a discussion of the concepts "basic thinking" and "complex-level thinking" and categories of thinking associated with the latter,

- a description of metacognition,

- a brief synopsis of the debate about the relationship between thinking skills and specific disciplines, and

- an overview of current programs and methods for teaching complex-level thinking.

TIME OUT. A quick disclaimer before proceeding. Please remember, we are providing you with a *simple* road map. The generalizations that are about to be made can be easily disputed. With any generalization, there is always the "but, but" or "how about . . ." However, we have attempted to avoid any protests and arguments with the adjectives "most" or "many."

Thinking

Before discussing how to *teach* thinking, we must understand what the term "thinking" means. Thinking can be defined in its simplest form as a series of activities the brain undergoes when presented with a stimulus. Stimuli are received through any of the five senses: touch, sight, sound, smell, or taste. Art Costa, author and editor of a number of books on thinking, explains that once we receive data, the information is processed into relationships that make sense—in short, "we think."[1]

The activity that the brain undergoes when thinking cannot be seen. Thinking, therefore, is an abstract concept, like justice or evil or power. You can't touch, feel, smell, or see an abstract construct—so, in a sense, thinking is not real! Then why is so much attention focused on it? Because what we see continually in our classrooms is the *result* of thinking—in other words, the output, in either oral, written, or kinesthetic form.

When viewing the thinking of students, we become fascinated with why some students have good problem-solving strategies and others don't, why some students make inferences and others can't. The innate intelligence of a child is only one piece of the puzzle. Other factors influence the capacity to think. The struggle, then, is to define and understand the bits and pieces that make up thinking—the action going on "behind the scenes." It is similar to the experience of tasting a delectable dish in a fancy restaurant and trying to figure out the ingredients.

Because the act of thinking cannot be directly observed, researchers have attempted to figure out the "ingredients" of thinking by first presenting a stimulus (or task) and then observing the resulting behaviors. These investigators have discovered that the more difficult (or abstract) a task is, the more complex the thinking processes required.

Some brief examples are in order. Basic cognitive tasks do not demand a great deal of mental activity. If someone asks you your name, you reply automatically. The mental process is so quick that you are not aware of any mental exertion. On the other hand, if someone asks you how the world would be different if there were no computers, you find yourself engaged in a more difficult mental exercise.

Based on the way people confront and handle various tasks, researchers and theorists have divided thinking into "lower-level" and "higher-level" categories. "Higher" and "lower" are unfortunate terms because they are value laden, suggesting that higher-level thinking is "better" than lower-level thinking. We prefer the terms "basic" and "complex" because they are more descriptive and less biased.

Basic- and Complex-Level Thinking

It is generally agreed that you need to master the more basic operations before you can operate at the more complex levels of thinking. You cannot coherently discuss the lack of computers in the world if you do not know what a computer is or the different ways that they are used.

So far, we can easily locate ourselves on the road map. We all agree that there are basic and complex thinking behaviors. Amazingly, there is even some consensus as to the types of thinking that belong in each category. The land of "basic-level thinking" contains memory, recall, basic comprehension, and observation skills.

Barry Beyer, one of the earliest leaders in the thinking skills movement, has summarized the consensus on complex-level thinking. "Most educators," Beyer notes, "agree that [complex-level] thinking skills (unlike social or psychomotor skills) are essentially mental techniques or abilities that enable human beings to formulate thoughts, to reason about, or to judge."[2] Richard Paul, another educator frequently associated with this field, has identified a number of characteristics of complex thinking:

+ it is nonalgorithmic (i.e., the path of action cannot be fully laid out before the problem),
+ it has multiple solutions,
+ it involves judgment,
+ it uses multiple criteria,
+ it is effortful, and
+ it imposes meaning.[3]

Most people acknowledge that at least three types of complex-level thinking are possible:

- ✦ critical thinking (sometimes called reasoning or evaluative thinking),

- ✦ creative thinking (sometimes called divergent thinking), and

- ✦ problem solving.

In addition to these three types of thinking, decision making is often suggested as a fourth category. Each type of thinking has a distinct set of skills or processes associated with it.

People frequently use the terms *skill* and *process*—often interchangeably—when discussing thinking. As with many other issues, little clarification is given as to the difference between the two. We will use *processes* to refer to the large categories of complex thinking we have listed above. Critical thinking, creative thinking, problem solving, and decision making are processes. *Skills*, on the other hand, are those specific abilities that are associated with each process. For example, making inferences, judging the credibility of a source, and making a generalization would be considered critical-thinking skills.

However, it would be simplistic to assume that thinking processes and skills are discrete functions. The nature of complex thinking is such that when you are thinking critically, you are also using some creative and problem-solving techniques. That is why this type of thinking is called complex!

Although most researchers agree on the three or four types of thinking, trouble starts when they build their individual models of thinking skills from this accumulated common knowledge.* Unfortunately, the many education "cartographers" have been trained at different schools and consequently have drawn many disparate maps. The geography of complex thinking changes from person to person, locations vary from map to map, and similar locations often have dissimilar signposts marking them. These disparities among models can be seen in the differing vocabularies used to describe the various skills or processes as well as in the varying emphases.

For instance, some might argue that critical thinking is the broad category of thinking that encompasses all other types; for others, problem solving is seen as the "umbrella" for all complex mental processes. How the relationship of critical thinking to creative thinking is viewed varies as well, depending on who is having the discussion.

---

*The term *model* refers to a complete verbal representation of ideas and theories.

In this chapter, we summarize the common strands in the definitions of critical thinking, creative thinking, problem solving, and decision making. We then discuss metacognition and its role in the overall scheme. We will avoid presenting you with too many definitions; the result would be a confusing "mess" of words and ideas that can be overwhelming to anyone first exploring this field. However, for those who want to delve deeper, we will cite a few references.

Critical Thinking

The type of complex thinking discussed most often is critical thinking. Of particular importance are definitions suggested by a number of individuals currently associated with the thinking field: Barry Beyer, Deborah Burns, Art Costa and Barbara Presseisen, Robert Ennis, Shirley Schiever, and Robert Sternberg.[4]

In analyzing the varied definitions suggested by these researchers, some common characteristics appear:

- ✦ critical thinking requires more than the "comparatively" simple process of remembering something and involves a degree of skill;

- ✦ critical thinking involves an element of judgment on the part of the thinker;

- ✦ critical thinking involves a degree of logic and systematic reasoning (in comparison to creative thinking); and

- ✦ unlike problem solving and decision making, critical thinking is not defined as a series of steps but rather as a set of skills.

Creative Thinking

Paul E. Torrance, one of the better-known researchers in creativity, defines the creative process as "becoming sensitive to or aware of problems, deficiencies, gaps in knowledge, missing elements, disharmonies, and so on; bringing together in new relationships available existing information; . . . searching for solutions, making guesses, or formulating hypotheses about the problems."[5] Burns notes that individuals engage in a number of behaviors when thinking creatively, including judgment deferring, problem finding, attribute listing, and brainstorming. Other skills associated with creativity include risk taking, tolerance of ambiguity, and curiosity.[6] Torrance, as well as many other researchers and theorists in the area of creativity, suggests that creative products have four basic components: flexibility, originality, fluency, and elaboration.[7]

Critical thinking implies a degree of logic, rationality, and some linearity. In contrast, creative thinking is nonrational and illogical. Yet some researchers suggest that the two types of thinking are complementary and actually overlap in some areas. As Marzano et al. state: "Distinguishing between them [critical and creative thinking] is impossible because all good thinking involves both quality assessment and the production of novelty. Critical thinkers generate ways to test assertions; creative thinkers examine newly generated thoughts to assess their validity and utility. The difference is not of kind but of degree and emphasis."[8] We believe that it is difficult to engage in one process without help from the other, but the outcome of your thinking will vary depending on whether the task primarily demands creative or critical thinking.

Problem Solving

All types of complex thinking involve a "problem" and various methods of solving it. In a general sense, then, problem solving is a part of all complex cognition. However, problem solving, when used to refer to a specific category of thinking, refers to a sequential process for solving an identified problem. The definitions of problem solving suggested by Beyer, Costa and Presseisen, and Parnes have the following elements in common: [9]

+ a series of steps, usually starting with a definition of the problem;

+ a degree of creativity in suggesting possible solutions; and

+ selection of a solution, execution of the solution, and evaluation of the results.

Problem solving, unlike critical thinking and creativity, lends itself more naturally to teaching because steps, not skills, are emphasized.

Decision Making

Decision making is considered by some to be a separate type of thinking. The definition of decision making is implied in the term: decision making is the process of making, or arriving at, a decision. Many individuals believe decision making is a key skill we use throughout our lives.[10] However, as in other definitions, specific interpretations of decision making vary from individual to individual.

Most useful definitions of decision making contain the following components:

+ a series of steps,

+ the generation of alternative decisions, and

+ an assessment of the alternatives using preselected criteria.

In reviewing the definitions of problem solving and decision making, several strong similarities become evident. Both definitions contain steps, starting with some type of problem and resulting in a solution. Various solutions are evaluated by selected criteria, resulting in a final decision.

The major difference between problem solving and decision making is in the perception of the solution. In problem solving, one begins without an answer and attempts to arrive at a workable, adequate solution to a problem; in decision making, one might begin with possible solutions. Therefore, adequate is not enough: decision makers must weigh various options to arrive at the best one for their goals.[11]

Teaching students to make decisions is important; however, to be perfectly honest, we don't believe the case has been made convincingly that a clear distinction exists between problem solving and decision making, particularly for the pragmatic demands of the classroom. In other words, you can teach decision making using a problem-solving model if you so desire.

Metacognition

When students verbalize what is going on mentally before, during, or after the thinking process, they are engaging in metacognition; in other words, metacognition is the thinking we do about our own thinking. It can be defined more precisely: "Metacognition is our ability to formulate a plan of action, monitor our own progress along that plan, realize what we know and don't know, detect and recover from error, and reflect upon and evaluate our own thinking processes."[12] Sometimes metacognition has been referred to as "reflection," "executive processes," or "executive functions."

The types of thinking previously discussed—critical, creative, problem solving, and decision making—are considered cognitive processes. Metacognition, on the other hand, is a process that can be used whether the student is thinking critically, solving problems, making decisions, or being creative. In other words, metacognition overshadows the other areas of thinking previously discussed and requires far more sophistication. It is a higher order of thought, requiring a strong degree of consciousness and awareness.

Because metacognition requires the ability to think abstractly, younger children have more difficulty learning metacognitive strategies. Developmentally, most individuals do not acquire the ability to think abstractly until the age of eleven, so metacognition is most successful with junior-high and high-school students. For elementary-age students, teaching premetacognitive strategies is useful (often referred to as learning-how-to-learn techniques).

Students, however, need more than the developmental ability to engage in metacognition. The ability to think about one's thinking requires certain preexisting attitudes and emotions. For example, students must feel capable of solving a problem and be motivated to approach it. Teachers can teach toward these necessary attitudes and emotions, just as they can teach specific metacognitive skills. In chapters 5 and 6, we will give specific suggestions for developing both the former and the latter strategies.

Metacognition, metacognitive strategies, and the disposition of the learner when engaging in them have received a tremendous amount of interest from cognitive psychologists and educators for a number of years. Researchers have studied the differences between poor learners and efficient learners, as well as the differences between novices and experts in certain fields. They have found that awareness of one's mental process leads to more efficient problem solving and reading.[13] As Costa puts it: "Evidently, thinking and talking about thinking beget more thinking."[14]

As with the other processes we have discussed, everyone has a slightly different concept of the components of metacognition. However, there are a number of skills commonly associated with it:

+ planning an approach to a problem, *

+ selecting a strategy to use,

+ applying your strategy after selection,

+ monitoring your performance during problem solving, and

+ evaluating your performance after solving the problem.

Metacognitive skills can be applied before, during, or after a thinking exercise.

Our Road Map

As you can see from our discussion on the types of thinking processes and metacognition, the experts continue to argue about the structure of thinking skills and their relationship to each other. However, in order to teach thinking, you need a road map to find the way. Because you will not find only one road map, you must select one from the many offered. Table 1 on page 28 gives the definitions we use in the book for the terms "complex-level thinking," "critical thinking," "creative thinking," and "problem solving." Complex-level thinking is the overall term that encompasses all higher-level processes. Critical thinking, creative thinking, and problem solving are the three categories of complex thinking. Table 1 also contains the specific skills that are associated with each one of the thinking processes.

---

*When discussing metacognitive skills, *problem* refers to any thinking activity or discussion in which students are pondering an issue, a topic, or a dilemma. This use of the term *problem* is more generic than in discussions of problem solving, which refers to a specific set of steps one undertakes to eliminate a particular obstacle.

TABLE 1
Complex-Level Thinking Skills*

Complex-Level Thinking: A type of cognition that requires basic thinking and is characterized by multiple possible answers, judgment on the part of the person participating, and the imposition of meaning on a situation. Types of complex thinking include critical thinking, creative thinking, and problem solving.

CRITICAL THINKING

A type of complex-level thinking characterized by the careful analysis of arguments, use of objective criteria, and evaluation of data.

1. Inductive thinking skills
- ➤ Determining cause and effect
- ➤ Analyzing open-ended problems
- ➤ Reasoning by analogy
- ➤ Making inferences
- ➤ Determining relevant information
- ➤ Recognizing relationships
- ➤ Solving insight problems

2. Deductive thinking skills
- ➤ Using logic
- ➤ Spotting contradictory statements
- ➤ Analyzing syllogisms
- ➤ Solving spatial problems

3. Evaluative thinking skills
- ➤ Distinguishing between facts and opinions
- ➤ Judging credibility of a source
- ➤ Observing and judging observation reports
- ➤ Identifying central issues and problems
- ➤ Recognizing underlying assumptions
- ➤ Detecting bias, stereotypes, cliches
- ➤ Recognizing loaded language
- ➤ Evaluating hypotheses
- ➤ Classifying data
- ➤ Predicting consequences
- ➤ Demonstrating sequential synthesis of information
- ➤ Planning alternative strategies
- ➤ Recognizing inconsistencies in information
- ➤ Identifying stated and unstated reasons
- ➤ Comparing similarities and differences
- ➤ Evaluating arguments

CREATIVE THINKING

A type of complex-level thinking that produces new and original ideas.

- ➤ Listing attributes of objects/situations
- ➤ Generating multiple ideas (fluency)
- ➤ Generating different ideas (flexibility)
- ➤ Generating unique ideas (originality)
- ➤ Generating detailed ideas (elaboration)
- ➤ Synthesizing information

PROBLEM SOLVING

A type of complex-level thinking that uses a number of sequential skills to solve a problem.

- ➤ Identifying general problem
- ➤ Clarifying problem
- ➤ Formulating hypothesis
- ➤ Formulating appropriate questions
- ➤ Generating related ideas
- ➤ Formulating alternative solutions
- ➤ Choosing best solution
- ➤ Applying the solution
- ➤ Monitoring acceptance of the solution
- ➤ Drawing conclusions

*Adapted from Gubbin's Matrix of Thinking Skills. Gubbin's Matrix compiles and distills ideas from Bloom, Bransford, Bruner, Carpenter, Dewey, Ennis, Feuerstein, Jones, Kurfman, Kurfman and Solomon, Lipman, Orlandi, Parnes, Paul, Perkins, Renzulli, Sternberg, Suchman, Taba, Torrence, Upton, The Ross Test, the Whimbey Analytical Skills Test, The Cornell Critical Thinking Test, the Cognitive Abilities Test, the Watson-Glasser Critical Thinking Appraisal, the New Jersey Test of Reasoning Skills, and the SEA Test.

Table 2 defines metacognition as we will refer to it and lists strategies and skills associated with it.

Table 2
Sample List of Metacognitive Skills

Metacognition: The consciousness of one's own thinking processes before, during, or following a complex-level thinking session.

KNOWLEDGE AND CONTROL OF ONESELF

Attitudes
This component includes such characteristics as
learning from failure and belief in oneself.

Attention
This component includes the knowledge that different tasks require
different attention levels, the ability to control our attention,
and the use of selective attention skills.

Commitment
This component includes the ability to stay with a task even when it is difficult.

KNOWLEDGE AND CONTROL OF PROCESS

Planning
This component involves the deliberate selection of a strategy
or plan of action prior to the activity.

Applying
This component involves the application of the selected strategy.

Regulating and Monitoring
This component involves checking your progress toward your intended goal.
It also includes the ability to change or adapt your strategy as necessary.

Evaluation
This component involves determining the success or failure of your strategy
and also assessing your current knowledge state.

This table compiles ideas from various sources including E. Bondy, "Thinking about Thinking," *Childhood Education* (March/April 1984): 234-38, and R.J. Marzano et al., *Dimensions of Thinking: A Framework for Curriculum and Instruction* (Alexandria, Va.: Association for Supervision and Curriculum Development).

Once you have a road map for use, there are other issues to contemplate before teaching. A major one focuses on the relationship of thinking to content areas.

The Match between Content and Thinking Processes: Thinking Skills within the Disciplines

Perhaps one of the biggest areas of dispute right now in the thinking field centers around the question of "subject specificity."[15] In other words, do individual disciplines (e.g., math, science, social sciences, language arts) have certain types of thinking processes associated exclusively with them? For example, does a student use a set of thinking skills specific to science when studying science and then another set of skills when studying language arts?

Also receiving considerable attention is a related question: Can general thinking skills be taught across all disciplines, and furthermore, will students transfer their use of a skill in one discipline to another discipline? Let's elaborate on the previous example: Can the same student learn a set of general thinking skills in science that he or she will then use when studying language arts? A third question in this debate combines the earlier two: Are there thinking skills specific to each discipline as well as thinking skills that can be used in all disciplines?

The relationship of subject specificity to metacognition has also been explored. We know that metacognition—thinking about thinking—can be employed regardless of the discipline or thinking process being taught. However, do metacognitive strategies exist that are subject-matter and/or situation specific? In simpler words, do certain metacognitive strategies work in only certain disciplines, and are there general metacognitive strategies to use in all areas of study as well?

By this point, you should be getting used to the fact that the numerous questions surrounding the topic of thinking and the teaching of thinking have few definitive answers. Such is true on the question of subject specificity. Still, researchers and theorists have suggested a number of possible theories. For example, David Perkins, one of the people most interested in this topic, and Gavriel Salomon have hypothesized a synthesis to the disagreement about subject specificity. In brief, what Perkins and Salomon say is: "There are general cognitive skills; but they always function in contextualized ways."[16] They then outline the basic components of their position. Although arguments will continue to abound over thinking skills in content areas, Perkins and Salomon have gone a long way to resolve some of the questions.

The questions surrounding subject specificity and the other issues raised in this chapter are serious and important ones. People far more qualified than we are actively pursuing solutions. In time, their explorations should provide more insight into the dilemmas. We applaud their efforts and look forward to clearer resolution. However, the lack of agreement doesn't mean thinking can't be taught.

The Teaching of Thinking

Instrumental Enrichment. Tactics for Thinking. Project Intelligence. CoRT. Philosophy for Children. Structure of the Intellect. HOTS. Chances are that you have heard of at least one of these thinking programs. A bewildering number of programs and materials are available for teaching students and adults how to think better. Some approaches are better known than others, but all of them purport to teach students how to improve their ability to think. Nickerson, Perkins, and Smith have listed a number of areas in which thinking-skills programs differ: [17]

+ scope,
+ specific skills addressed,
+ amount of training needed,
+ ages and academic abilities of students,
+ type of material,
+ research evidence for effectiveness, and
+ degree of integration with other courses.

In addition, Robert Baum notes that some programs are infused in the curriculum, while others are separate from the curriculum.[18] Individuals must ask which approach they prefer. Complete overviews of thinking programs can be found in a number of resources.[19]

Regardless of the differences among programs, a key assumption of every thinking skills program is that *all* students, regardless of intelligence or home environment, can improve their thinking. Very few people (at least publicly) will say that only gifted students can improve their thinking. The quality and quantity of thinking will vary from student group to student group, but all students can become better thinkers.

We don't know which programs work and which do not. Data have been difficult to collect for a number of reasons, including the newness of the programs, difficulty in assessing thinking, poor research design, lack of outside evaluations, and conflicting results.

In fact, it is not even our goal to recommend thinking-skills programs. Consult any of the researchers mentioned in this chapter for help in selecting a program for your classroom or school. However, if you are considering purchasing a program, it would be wise to ask a number of questions first:

+ Can we afford the time and money this program requires?
+ Do we agree with the basic philosophy of the program?
+ Does the program teach the thinking skills that are emphasized, either overtly or covertly, in our curriculum?
+ Can the program be integrated easily into our curriculum?

Conclusion

We have taken you on a quick tour through the thinking world landscape using other people's maps. Some details on the landscape are clear and others remain shrouded in fog. As you explore this new area, you will become more familiar with many of the names and concepts we have summarized. Yet this information is only a prelude to the real purpose of our book—to show you how you can make your own journey toward the thoughtful classroom *without* a prepackaged program or published materials.

4

The Thoughtful Classroom:
Packing for the Journey

Thinking is like living and dying: you must do it for yourself.

Anonymous

Teachers who are interested in the journey toward the thoughtful classroom may be faced with a number of curriculum options:

✦ a district-adopted thinking curriculum is being used or considered for use,

✦ a commercial program is being used or considered for use, or

✦ financial resources or professional support to implement a prepackaged program is lacking, but interest is strong in teaching complex-level thinking.

In all three cases, a commitment has been made to build the thoughtful classroom—a community of disciplined inquiry where both students and teachers value complex thinking and regularly engage in thoughtful discourse.

Items you pack must be carefully selected.

However, completing a journey of this nature takes more than commitment. The items you pack must be carefully selected. Two articles are crucial. The first article to ensure success is establishing a classroom climate that fosters and values complex thinking. This climate is a precursor to the implementation of any thinking-skills curriculum. Once this classroom environment is in place, the second article can be packed—the regular, planned teaching of thinking. This systematic teaching, in whatever form, is the primary means for teaching students to think, and it involves a number of elements: teachers must plan lessons, find time for teaching the material, and evaluate the success of the lessons. (If a commercial or already established curriculum is being used, the first element may already be given. If a prepackaged curriculum is not being employed, then the teacher is responsible for selecting, designing, and implementing the material.)

In this chapter, we take a closer look at the two articles. First, we will discuss the necessary classroom environment that fosters complex thinking. This discussion should be of interest to all teachers: regardless of your curriculum, every teacher needs to maintain a classroom atmosphere that values thinking.*

In the second half of the chapter, we will look at the thinking lesson and its components. A possible framework for planning and teaching complex-thinking lessons will be suggested. We will briefly discuss the actual teaching and evaluation of the lesson at the end of the chapter. This section will be of primary interest to those teachers who do not have the financial resources or professional support to implement a prepackaged program.**

The First Article to Pack:
A Classroom Environment that Fosters Complex Thinking

Before all else, a classroom environment that fosters complex thinking must be predictable and safe. Thinking can be encouraged in such an atmosphere only. Few students will venture to verbalize a thought or challenge the teacher or a peer if he or she risks being ridiculed or ignored.

A major part of a safe and predictable environment is having established routines. It can take several years to learn how to implement regular classroom procedures, including such familiar problems as keeping students on task, handling paperwork, meeting state and district curriculum mandates, and maintaining discipline. Yet implementing and maintaining a set routine is an important precursor to teaching thinking.

How do you know if your classroom is safe and predictable? We have provided a list of questions concerning the classroom climate. "Yes" answers indicate a safe classroom environment. Go ahead and assess yourself.

---

*Although the term *curriculum* is a broad and rather complex concept, for the purpose of our discussion, we will be using it in a much simpler way. By curriculum, we are referring to the course of study that is covered in your classroom. Curriculum is often mandated at a state or local level, with goals and objectives described and distributed in written form. Teachers accomplish these goals and objectives through the use of a variety of teaching strategies.

**This chapter is really an introduction to chapters 5, 6, 7, and 8; most of the material in this chapter will be elaborated on in those chapters.

- ◆ Are there safeguards for the physically vulnerable child (e.g., adequate adult supervision and orderly procedures for moving children and selecting groups)?
- ◆ Are there safeguards for the psychologically vulnerable child (e.g., clear classroom procedures for dealing with verbal or physical abuse)?
- ◆ Is there an agreement, written or unwritten, that all people and their ideas are treated with respect?
- ◆ Do I model respect in my interaction with *all* students and other teachers?
- ◆ Are students on task in the classroom?
- ◆ Do students accept mistakes by themselves or others as mechanisms for learning?
- ◆ Do students realize that learning is valued?
- ◆ Do students know the consequences of their actions with a clear, *consistent* discipline procedure in place?
- ◆ Do my students see me as predictable and consistent, and do my students trust me ("trust" is not necessarily synonymous with "like")?

If you answer yes to these questions, you have a safe, predictable classroom climate—and, most likely, several years of teaching already behind you.

Experience is an invaluable guide. So, to the new teacher reading this book we offer a caution. Given that you will be "learning the ropes" and trying to teach thinking at the same time, start very small. Give yourself a chance to establish the daily, necessary routines. Numerous books already exist that will provide you with details on how to organize and efficiently run a classroom as well as create a secure classroom environment.[1] Read them *and* our book, and pick out the recommendations that seem easiest. With each year, you will gain more confidence and can attempt more challenges.

An environment that fosters complex thinking will be safe and predictable, but there is an even more important component: the belief that thinking is essential, valued, and enjoyable. Many teachers have safe classroom environments but do not value complex thinking. These classrooms are characterized by large amounts of teacher direction, teacher talk, and basic skills. The teacher is the authority in most matters. On the other hand, a classroom that values thinking is characterized by shared decision making when appropriate, a lively exchange of opinions and ideas, and visual evidence of student thinking.

The belief that thinking is important cannot be instilled simply by reading a book or two on the subject. We acquire it through many complex and intricate forces that operate on each of us. In short, we value thinking if those "significant others" around us taught us to do so.

If you esteem thinking—and we assume you do—the next step is to impart this belief to your students as much as possible. Rarely will students value complex thinking spontaneously. They must be trained to appreciate thinking in themselves, their peers, and their teachers. Students learn to prize complex-level thinking by observing the teacher exhibit a variety of behaviors in both informal and formal settings. Solving classroom problems with students openly (e.g., "How are we going to keep the room clean?") and finding spontaneous opportunities to think with kids are two examples of informal ways in which teachers demonstrate that thinking is an important part of the classroom.

A Safe and Predictable Environment

How do you know if your classroom is safe and predictable? Answer these questions concerning the classroom climate. Yes answers indicate a safe classroom environment.

	YES	NO
1. Can a child tell you the probable routine for the day?	❏	❏
2. Does planning occur with the students as to the order of the day's activities?	❏	❏
3. Safeguards for the physically vulnerable child:		
Is there adequate adult supervision at all times?	❏	❏
Is there adult supervised movement of groups of children?	❏	❏
Is there adult supervised selection of groups?	❏	❏
4. Safeguards for the psychologically vulnerable child:		
Are there procedures to deal with verbal abuse among peers?	❏	❏
Are there procedures to deal with physical abuse among peers?	❏	❏
5. Is the discipline plan known to students, parents, and administrators?	❏	❏
Is it clear?	❏	❏
Are the consequences clear?	❏	❏
Are the rules few?	❏	❏
Are the rules fair and firmly enacted?	❏	❏
6. Does the teacher model respect for ALL students in the group?	❏	❏
7. Does the teacher model respect for all student IDEAS in the group?	❏	❏
8. Is the humor used respectful?	❏	❏
9. Are the tasks asked of the students purposeful? (That is, can children tell a stranger WHY they are performing a certain task?)	❏	❏
10. Are students on task in the classroom?	❏	❏
11. Does the teacher model a learning person as well as a teaching one?	❏	❏
12. Does the teacher model mistakes as tools for learning?	❏	❏
13. Would the student say YES to:		
My teacher says what she/he means.	❏	❏
My teacher means what she/he says.	❏	❏
My teacher believes I can learn.	❏	❏
My teacher is fair.	❏	❏
My teacher can be trusted.	❏	❏

However, teachers have a far more dramatic impact on students in structured, planned settings. These can include regular lessons or classroom meetings. The formal setting we discuss in the next section is the one that occurs when teachers teach systematic, regular thinking lessons.

The Second Article to Pack: The Thinking Lesson

Complex-level thinking is developed in students primarily through the careful planning and teaching of lessons. A lesson, as we use the term here, encompasses more than assigned pages in the math book. A lesson is any designated activity that has one or more specific objectives the teacher hopes to accomplish. If one objective of a lesson is the teaching of a thinking skill, it can be considered a complex-thinking lesson.

In chapter 2, we advocated the use of the conceptual infusion method for teaching thinking, wherein the teacher integrates both thinking and content into the lesson. A lesson using the infused method must meet certain criteria. First, lessons need to be structured so that students think actively. Second, students must be aware of the thinking they are doing. Although content and process are blended together, the complex-level thinking skills being taught are explicitly labeled for the students before, during, and after the lesson. Finally, the lesson must allow students different opportunities to practice applying the thinking skill.[2]

Teachers must find the right balance between content and process—not overwhelming students by teaching new, unfamiliar content while also requiring complex-level thinking. Meeting both the objectives of teaching content and teaching thinking processes can be achieved by the careful, sequential planning of the thinking lessons.

Planning a Complex-Level Thinking Lesson

Much of the work in teaching a complex-level thinking lesson must come *before* the lesson.* In fact, planning is particularly necessary because there are too many opportunities to go astray or crash on the rocks. A teacher needs to have the wheel firmly in hand to keep thirty or more minds on course. Students will offer great (and not so great) ideas and wonderful (and not so wonderful) insights that may not be relevant.

Using a systematic format will greatly improve your chances of having a classroom of thinkers. We propose a six-step process for planning a thinking lesson:

---

*If you are using a commercial or already written curriculum, the planning of lessons may have been done for you, which will save you a considerable amount of time and energy.

1. Identify the content area in which the lesson will be taught.

2. Identify the complex-level thinking strategies you wish to emphasize.

3. Identify the teacher strategies you wish to emphasize.

4. Identify the student behaviors you wish to encourage in your students.

5. Make a commitment to an overarching concept or idea for the lesson.

6. Outline the progression of the lesson in detail.

You might find that you don't plan in this sequence (one of us doesn't either). Don't worry—find the order that works for you. The key is to end up with a lesson plan that covers the six steps.

1—Identify the content area in which the lesson will be taught.

Thinking does not occur in isolation; you must think *about* something. Nickerson states that thinking is a "totally knowledge-dependent activity; to think, one must think about something. Other things being equal, the more one knows, the more effective one's thinking is likely to be. Much knowledge does not guarantee effective thinking, but lack of knowledge surely prohibits it."[3] In other words, the teacher must have content for the lesson to occur.

How does a teacher identify the content area in which the lesson will be taught? Our preference is clear: the content for a complex-thinking lesson needs to arise naturally from the classroom curriculum. In other words, a thinking lesson should occur in "situated learning," not as an isolated workbook page, separate from the classroom activities. When identifying content for a thinking lesson, look to your classroom curriculum. Remember that curriculum can include the content of textbooks as well other materials. Topics or problems that do not require "right answers" are appropriate. For example, current events, "hands-on" science experiments, or literature-based reading discussions provide suitable content.

For most teachers, selecting the appropriate content is easy. Traditional teacher training is oriented toward content methodology; the result is that most of us are very comfortable with locating relevant material. Keep in mind, however, that both the type of lesson and the thinking skills already demonstrated by the students will determine the depth and type of content. Students do not need a lot of content to think on complex levels. However, the more students know, the more sophisticated their thinking will be.

2—Identify the complex-level thinking strategy(ies) you wish to emphasize.

Once you identify the content you are going to use, the next step is to figure out what thinking process can be developed within the lesson. As noted in the previous chapter, the complex-level strategies you select may come from a number of sources. Some of you will already have chosen thinking processes and skills to use.* For others, Tables 1 and 2 in chapter 3 (see pages 28 and 29) can be employed when identifying the complex-level thinking processes and skills you wish to teach.

When developing a complex-thinking lesson, the teacher must ask: What are the thinking skill(s) I wish to teach? Our experience has been that answering this question is often the most difficult part of planning. Many of us are comfortable with stating, "I'm teaching a critical-thinking lesson." Most often we are teaching thinking, and yet, do we know which specific skill(s) the lesson will reinforce or develop?

In the early stages of developing the thoughtful classroom, setting the tone is fine. Being aware of the difference between a thoughtful and a nonthoughtful classroom and trying some new things is the important part. Teaching "general" complex thinking on a regular basis is far more vital than being able to identify specific skills in your lesson plan. However, as you become more familiar with the planning and teaching of thinking lessons, eventually you will need to know what skills or processes you are teaching.

Teachers have a difficult time identifying specific thinking skills to emphasize because the terminology and language is often unfamiliar and abstract; consequently teachers can be uneasy and at a loss as to how to select thinking skills. We did an exercise with the teachers in the Creating the Thoughtful Classroom project to confront this problem. The teachers, in small groups, looked at the thinking skills listed in the table on page 28 and then generated examples of how each skill is used by students during classroom activities. Teachers quickly discovered that many of the concepts were familiar if they would simply take time to think about each one.

When you are ready to identify specific thinking skills in your lesson plan, focus on one skill within a certain process. For example, teach only how to make inferences. Select a skill that you are naturally comfortable with and understand conceptually. Trying to teach more than one skill will be difficult, particularly if you are just beginning to try some of these ideas. The nature of complex thinking is such that when you are teaching one thinking skill, many other thinking skills will be reinforced as well. However, having one focus makes evaluation much easier.

---

*See chapter 3 and appendix A for sources.

After selecting the complex-level thinking skills and the content you wish to use, the two components need to be integrated into one lesson. Although the first two steps are listed separately, the selection of one will influence the other. The type of content you use will be related to the thinking processes you select. For example, when teaching math concepts you might wish to use problem-solving skills as your thinking process. With language arts, critical or creative thinking may be your objective.

Furthermore, the difficulty of your content may influence the type of thinking you teach. "Easy" content may require less-demanding thinking skills. For example, when introducing a science unit on chemistry, a teacher might brainstorm everything students associate with the word *chemistry*.* Students can then classify ideas into categories, and the categories can be used for study or research topics. This activity requires easy content and the relatively easy skill of classification and concept development. Later on in the unit, when analyzing photosynthesis, for example, both the content and the thinking processes are more difficult.

3—Identify the teacher strategies you wish to emphasize.

The strategies the teacher uses during the lesson are a fundamental component of teaching complex-level thinking. These strategies include calling on all students to respond and waiting for students to think about a question. When teachers consistently model appropriate teacher strategies and behaviors, students quickly learn that thinking is a priority.

During the planning process, the teacher should select one or, at most, two strategies to focus on during the lesson. As you can imagine, concentrating on several strategies at a time can lead to disaster and frustration. Highlighting one or two specific strategies will lead to far greater success. In chapter 6, we will discuss nine crucial teacher strategies and ways to develop them.

4—Identify the student behaviors you wish to encourage in your students.

This step is nearly identical to the previous step, only now the teacher selects the behaviors that students will develop. Older students can select their own behaviors. The teacher can challenge students to use certain behaviors during thinking lessons. Student behaviors include participating, listening to each other, and asking questions. Students can experience both the challenge and the joy of thinking by practicing these behaviors on a regular basis. The same caution applies with this step: students should focus on only one or two behaviors at a time. In chapter 7, we will talk about nine student behaviors.

---

*Brainstorming is a technique that is commonly used to encourage new ideas. Students are given a topic or problem and asked to generate as many solutions as possible, using the following guidelines: (a) think of as many ideas as you can, (b) no criticism of anyone else's ideas, and (c) "piggyback" on others' ideas freely.

5—Make a commitment to an overarching concept or idea for the lesson.

Mentally explore the alternate routes your students might take. At this point in the lesson, you are attempting to identify the concepts that you want your students to grasp; in other words, you are introducing the "conceptual" of the conceptual-infusion approach. A thinking lesson without a conceptual goal can degenerate into an activity with little focus or purpose.

The concept or idea you select should be abstract and go beyond the usual objective(s) of learning basic facts and figures; consequently, your students will not grasp the complexities of the idea in one lesson. In fact, if your students do understand the identified overarching idea, your concept is probably not abstract enough. The purpose of selecting an overarching concept or idea is to direct your thinking toward complex levels and make you aware of where you want your students to go. You can then develop a series of lessons that lead to comprehension of the selected concept. Here are some examples of lessons and corresponding conceptual ideas you might teach toward.

◆ Lesson content: Myths and mythology from different cultures
   Overarching lesson concept: Humans develop explanations to understand their environment.

◆ Lesson content: The settlers in the Southwest
   Overarching lesson concept: All settlers throughout history share similar characteristics.

◆ Lesson content: Endangered species
   Overarching lesson concept: Living things are interdependent with one another and with their environment.

The writing of a concept objective can take practice, because you are required to think abstractly about the material you are teaching. Remember that an overarching concept is not a simple statement summarizing the content. An overarching concept is a broad, abstract idea. Ask yourself: What complex-level concepts or larger ideas do I want students to obtain? State your overarching concept in the form of a sentence before the lesson begins. Know ahead of time the acceptable lesson outcomes.

6—Outline the progression of the lesson in detail.

At this point, you are ready to outline the specific steps you will follow when teaching the lesson. We have used a five-step approach, using the acronym SEEED:

1. State that a lesson will occur that requires complex thinking. Identify the thinking skill that will be used and describe the selected teacher strategies and student behaviors. This announcement is crucial for setting the tone and the climate. If this step is done regularly, you will notice how your students mentally prepare themselves.

2. Encounter the problem with the students. Focus on the thinking problem or question in a way that motivates and interests your class in the upcoming lesson. A puzzle, an intriguing story, a challenging question, or a mystery object can all be used to "hook" students.

3. Establish a common knowledge base. This step might involve presenting new or reviewing old information. If students are familiar with the content, a review of basic facts or figures would be appropriate. If you are introducing a unit, students might receive new content. In short, the groundwork is being laid for complex thinking.

4. Engage students in the complex thinking task(s). The type of learning group and activity will vary, depending on the objectives of the lesson. Sometimes the discussion format will be appropriate; at other times the active learning/manipulation format will be used (see chapter 2 for descriptions).

5. Discuss insights or results from the lesson. This final phase is similar to the "cool down" period in sports, where one slows the rate of exercise without completely stopping. This stage can involve metacognition, sharing of insights, possible extensions into other realms related to the identified concept, the articulation of new, related problems or questions, and/or a summary of the lesson's content.

Page 43 summarizes the SEEED format and page 44 gives a sample lesson plan form. In chapter 5, we will give examples of planned thinking lessons in the various content areas.

Your next step is to teach the lesson by following your plan.

Steps in the Lesson

State that a thinking lesson will occur: _____

_____

_____

_____

_____

Encounter the problem with the students: _____

_____

_____

_____

_____

Establish a common knowledge base: _____

_____

_____

_____

_____

Engage in the thinking task: _____

_____

_____

_____

_____

Discuss the insights and results: _____

_____

_____

_____

_____

Complex-Level Thinking
Lesson Plan

NAME:_____ DATE: _____

Content: _____

_____

_____

_____

_____

Thinking Skills:_____

_____

_____

_____

_____

Teacher Strategies: _____

_____

_____

_____

_____

Student Behaviors: _____

_____

_____

_____

_____

Overarching Concept or Idea of the Lesson: _____

_____

_____

_____

_____

Teaching a Complex-Level Thinking Lesson

We assume that you will be teaching thinking lessons on a regular basis in your classroom. Setting aside a particular time or times during the week gives the message to you and your students that thinking is an important part of the class. During your regular lesson, follow the five SEEED steps described in the previous section.

Plant a SEEED
Teach a thinking lesson.

Remember that all the planning in the world will not completely prepare you. The actual teaching of a planned, complex-level lesson is the fun part of our profession. Like people, lessons are never alike. The nonalgorithmic nature of complex thinking means that we can never predict completely what our students will say or do. Sometimes in thinking lessons, students move in a totally uncharted direction and a "teachable moment" shows up. So you find yourself teaching a different lesson. Great!

Just like students, each teacher brings to the five-step process his or her own flesh and blood. Your age, temperament, teaching, and life experiences shape what you bring to the lesson. Be aware that you are a dynamic force and that you must focus on the lesson itself. It isn't enough for students to think about what you are saying; a thoughtful classroom has the teacher thinking *with* the students.

This dynamic interaction between the teacher and the students is what makes the learning and teaching process continually exciting and challenging for all of us involved in it. Although at first it is an exhausting endeavor to get the twenty-five or more minds to think with you, you will begin to have fun. Thoughtfulness has momentum. Once you start the ball rolling, it is difficult to stop. The thoughtful classroom begins to take on a life of its own.

Evaluation of a Thinking Lesson

Evaluation of the lesson is a key part of improving your teaching of thinking. We are speaking of evaluating yourself as you teach thinking in your classroom; administrative evaluation is a separate issue. Self-evaluation has a number of steps; the first is to accept the importance of assessment and realize that such a commitment will require time and effort. In other words, if you own the need, you produce the change.

The next step is to decide what you wish to improve. For example, you can evaluate the type of thinking your students engage in or the frequency of a teaching strategy you wish to increase. Such a decision is determined by your personal situation and your own needs.

No book can give a complete recipe for successful teaching. We can read and ponder all kinds of written material, but eventually we must plan a lesson and then teach it. At the end of the lesson, evaluate yourself with predetermined criteria. We will supply you with specific techniques in chapter 8; you will need to find a colleague to observe (or the audio equipment to record) and the time to evaluate the results.

Conclusion

The pragmatic realities of teaching preclude higher-level thinking from happening all the time—this goal is neither desirable nor possible. Yet, complex-level thinking can be increased in your classroom. If you have a classroom environment that is safe and values thinking, integration of content and process emerging naturally from your curriculum, specific teacher strategies and student behaviors, and a well-planned lesson, complex thinking will begin to occur on a systematic basis in your classroom. Let's explore sample lessons in the next chapter.

5

Infusing Thinking into Your Curriculum: Beginning the Journey

*I believe we must make thinking the main agenda of our schools,
and that won't happen unless teachers are expected to think.*

Lauren Resnick

When discussing the teaching of thinking, people argue about such issues as the type and amount of content and whether thinking should be a separate course or part of the regular curriculum. In chapter 2, we discussed some of these arguments and presented a continuum of approaches (see pages 15-16). These methods of teaching thinking skills ranged from their total immersion in to their total separation from the regular curriculum.

Which method works within
the pragmatic demands
of my classroom?

Few solid facts exist to support any of the proposed teaching techniques. Therefore, when deciding the best way to teach thinking, teachers are forced to ask the age-old question, Which method works best within the pragmatic demands of the classroom? We have answered this question for ourselves by using the conceptual-infusion approach in our classrooms. The practitioners of this approach teach thinking skills as part of the regular curriculum but directly identify the thinking skills during the teaching of material. Specifically, content is selected from the designated curriculum and is taught in such a way as to require students to think about the material in a sophisticated manner.

In this chapter, we will expand on the ideas presented in chapter 4. Specifically, we will discuss:

◆ a rationale for using the conceptual-infusion approach,

◆ the current practices of infusion,

47

♦ the role of the thinking lesson in promoting the infusion of thinking,

♦ the restructuring of various types of classroom material into conceptual lessons (with examples of specific lessons), and

♦ the relation of individual thinking lessons to each other.

A Rationale for Using the Conceptual-Infusion Approach

We recommend the use of the conceptual-infusion approach for a number of reasons. Many teachers lack either the time, the training, or the materials to teach thinking separately. Teaching thinking as part of the regular curriculum is the only option most of us have. The conceptual-infusion approach allows flexibility in scheduling and lessons. Also, this method can be adapted to any teaching style or curriculum requirements.

Furthermore, if you use this infusion technique, old teaching approaches to content can be discarded. Content is no longer taught as a set of discrete facts; instead, the emphasis is placed on teaching "big ideas" and concepts. Teaching in an interdisciplinary manner results naturally from such a conceptual approach. Interdisciplinary teaching is efficient and exciting, while mirroring "real-world" content.

Finally, this method allows us the opportunity to teach students "real-world" problem-solving skills because thinking problems are presented much as adults face them. When encountering a difficult problem requiring complex-level thinking, adults do not stop to ponder which thinking skill is required (e.g., "Let me think for a moment—does this request from my boss for new investment trends require making inferences or cause-and-effect skills?"). Instead, the problem itself suggests possible avenues for solving it (e.g., "I need to analyze the trends for the past several months and then read the newest financial reports"). We automatically apply our thinking ability (to varying degrees) to the situation. In the real world, as in the conceptual-infusion method, content and process blend together.

In summary, then, using the conceptual-infusion approach can accomplish a number of important educational goals. First, students learn to think more and better. Also, the major disciplines—science, social studies, language arts, and math—are taught in a conceptual, and often interdisciplinary, manner. Finally, the thinking skills are acquired in such a manner that students are prepared for the future demands of their society.

Accepting the validity of the conceptual-infusion approach is only a small part of the battle; the larger one is how to integrate such an approach in the classroom. Current practices are not very successful.

Current Practices for Infusing Thinking into the Classroom

Increasingly, state and local school district curriculums are listing the attainment of complex-level thinking as a major objective. Yet, by and large, the materials available to teachers for reaching established goals, such as textbooks, trade books (i.e., books obtainable in the library), and nonprint materials, do not emphasize complex-level thinking. Therefore, the teacher is placed in a bind: mandated to teach complex-level thinking, yet having little access to published materials that will help achieve the directive.

Many teachers have "resolved" this dilemma by integrating a number of activities into their daily routine that require little planning or effort. For example, a teacher might:

+ add questions to textbooks that lack complex-level ones at the end of the reading,

+ ask for student opinions about a current event,

+ have classroom meetings and elections,

+ give students a "think problem" from commercially available "activity sheets" at the start of the day or use "one-time" sheets during other times,

+ talk about the importance of thinking on a regular basis,

+ brainstorm answers to a problem such as "How many different ways could I use this eraser?",

+ post signs in the classroom about thinking and its importance, and/or

+ talk about how important thinking is and how everyone in the class is a thinker.

If you take a moment to think about your day, you will identify other ways you encourage complex-level thinking in your classroom. We applaud these efforts and others that encourage more thinking in the classroom;[1] however, few of them would qualify as infusion techniques. Teaching an isolated lesson or two is not infusing, however strong and directed the instruction might be. Using occasional pages from workbooks or even a systematic thinking program, separate from your regular curriculum, is not infusing. Infusing implies the injection of complex-thinking activities into your classroom curriculum in a uniform and consistent manner.

The activities listed above are "content free." In other words, they do little to develop the "conceptual" side of the conceptual-infusion approach. Students may think on more complex levels when engaging in these activities, but the long-term value of such assignments can be questioned. These strategies are also isolated and do not fully integrate complex-level thinking into the classroom. More consistent action is needed to encourage sophisticated thinking across the curriculum.

Infusing Thinking into the Classroom Curriculum:
The Role of the Thinking Lesson

If you are to truly infuse thinking into your curriculum, you need to go beyond the worksheets and isolated lessons. You must start by defining for yourself what the integration of thinking would look like to you in your class. We approached this problem by first clarifying our conception of the thoughtful classroom (covered in previous chapters). In short, we wanted our students to have planned and well-thought-out opportunities for thinking on a daily basis. What we asked our students to think about would be a relevant part of our curriculum and would "fit" with our objectives. In addition, these opportunities needed to relate to each other and have internal consistency. In other words, occasions to think in one area of the curriculum would complement thinking activities in other domains.

Once you have a "vision" (use your own or share ours with us), turn a critical eye on what and how you are teaching. Where can you begin to infuse thinking? Find areas of the curriculum that interest you and lend themselves to complex-level thinking activities. Then, select the areas where you would be most willing to try some new ideas.

We have already stated that we believe the most consistent way to integrate conceptual thinking into the curriculum is through the regular teaching of thinking lessons.* These lessons, however, should not be isolated events; they need to fit together into the defined picture of a thoughtful classroom. The eventual goal would be the development of a comprehensive thinking curriculum, but first we can discuss in detail the specific components of the thinking lesson.

A well-designed thinking lesson has the components mentioned in chapter 4: selected content and thinking skills, identified teacher strategies and student behaviors, an overarching concept, and the SEEED outline. However, because each teaching situation is influenced by a number of important factors such as age of the students, amount of class time, student abilities, and personal teaching style, lessons developed by teachers will be highly individualized, reflecting these different influences as well as personal interests, skills, and experiences.

---

*Given the fact that a solid, complex-level thinking lesson requires time for both planning and teaching, teaching a thinking lesson daily is difficult. Realistically, teaching more than one SEEED lesson a week will be hard, particularly if you are just starting to consciously integrate thinking activities into your curriculum. However, as you develop weekly thinking lessons and exchange those with others from your colleagues, you will eventually have the option of teaching more than one fully developed lesson a week.

Both the problem and the attraction of the conceptual-infusion approach are in its flexibility. The method can be adapted to any curriculum, but *you* must do the adapting and, then, the "infusing." No one can provide you with a cookbook of specific, ready-to-use lessons for implementing the conceptual-infusion approach. In most instances, commercial materials that do have prepared lessons are limited in their use until the teacher adapts them to the particular situation. In sum, then, if you are going to teach thinking conceptually, you will have to develop your own lessons.

However, books such as ours can provide you with a springboard for your own creativity and imagination by suggesting various ways you might design and teach your thinking lessons.[2] One very important method you can use when developing thinking lessons is to restructure available material to fit the objectives of your lesson.

Restructuring Material

The goal of restructuring is to redesign your current material in such a way that when it is used, complex-level thinking will be encouraged. The process of restructuring requires complex-level thinking on the part of the designer; in many ways, this task requires the kind of critical and creative thinking we are advocating for our students. As you restructure your classroom materials, you will be astounded at the mental demand it requires. However, the challenge is fun and rewarding! Regardless of the material you select, initially, you need to decide:

+ what are the thinking skills you want to teach,
+ what content do you want to use to teach these thinking skills, and
+ what is the overarching idea you want your students to attain?

As we mentioned in chapter 4, you don't have to make all these decisions in the order listed. For example, you may be struck by an interesting section in the textbook and decide to use that material for a thinking lesson, *or* you might know what thinking skill you want to teach beforehand and actively seek some content to develop it.

Once you have determined these components, outline the lesson using the SEEED format. As you design the lesson, the material you are using can be restructured in any of these four ways to meet the identified objectives:

+ Use only a part of the material.
+ Use all the material, with specific focus on one part.
+ Use either all or only part, but have students apply only one sensory mode.
+ Use more than one type of material.

These four methods will be illustrated in the next section.

Curriculum materials available to teachers fall into three categories: nonprint media, textbooks, and trade books. We provide you with three sample SEEED lessons, one to complement each type of material.

Elementary Lesson: Restructuring Nonprint Media

Topic: Current Events in the Middle East

Background: This lesson was developed in response to the crisis in the Middle East caused by the Iraqi invasion of Kuwait. The fifth-grade teacher realized that she could not discuss the recent occurrences in the Middle East until her students understood the cultural influences in the area. Therefore, the first step was to explore the culture of the region. This sample lesson was one of a series and is shown on page 53.

As you can see by reading the lesson, the teacher has used a common teaching tool, the filmstrip, but restructured its use to promote the objectives of her lesson. Students view only a few frames of the filmstrip and are asked to focus their attention on those. Sound and narration are not used until the end of the lesson.

The lesson is a fairly simple one in the types of thinking it requires from students; however, a number of other, more complex lessons could develop from it. The filmstrip can be "revisited" for other lessons, too.

The lesson also illustrates how easily social studies can be used to teach complex-level thinking. Social studies has rich and vibrant content for students, whether you are studying ancient history, world history, Western civilization, or current events. The content allows you ample opportunity to infuse thinking. A number of resources might prove useful for you.[3]

Movies, videos, filmstrips, photographs, and slides are all examples of nonprint media that teachers employ regularly in the classroom. However, many times visual media are used indiscriminately or as a way to "fill time." Students often settle back in their chairs, knowing that little thinking will be required during *this* time. Remember, also, that the physical restraints on different types of media may determine their practical use in the classroom. For example, certain film projectors have a pause button to allow control over the roll. Many do not—the entire machine must be shut off in order to pause. Movie projectors also have a number of options, or restrictions, depending on the age and type. Know your hardware's capabilities when planning lessons.

RESTRUCTURING: Nonprint Media

Fifth-Grade Social Studies,
Culture of Saudi Arabia

State that a thinking lesson will occur:

"Today we are going to have a thinking lesson. I will be working on questioning skills and I would like you to work on participating. We are going to look at a filmstrip about the country of Saudi Arabia. First, you are going to make inferences based on pictures in the filmstrip, then we are going to categorize information from the filmstrip into four categories."

Encounter the problem with the students.

First, students are shown two frames without sound. Ask: *"What can you tell about their religion, based on these pictures?"* Allow time. Remind students: *"You must make an inference."*

Second, students are shown a set of four frames. Ask: *"What can you tell about women's roles in Saudi society based on these pictures?"* Repeat questions, using same frames re: government and economy.

Establish a common knowledge base.

After inferences are made for the four categories, the filmstrip is rewound and still with sound off, the teacher discusses student statements while frames are on screen. All students make statements. Answers written on the board. Each student chooses best answer for recording on chart (see below).

Engage in the thinking task.

Finally, the filmstrip is shown with sound. Students are requested to fill in information on their charts from information that was actually given in the filmstrip. Stop filmstrip when necessary for catch-up and writing.

Discuss the insights and results.

"What things in the pictures helped you infer correctly? Which things led you astray? What knowledge did you already have? What else might you want to know?"

Name:	Religion	Government	Economy	Role of Women
What I infer:				
What the filmstrip tells me:				

The goal, then, is to restructure audiovisual materials in such a way that students must now think and can no longer "kick back" during the movie. Nonprint media can be restructured in a number of ways similar to the example given. For example:

- ◆ Select only one or two frames that are most visually descriptive of the filmstrip's content. Show those parts to the students and have them make inferences about such things as the content of the picture. Use with or without sound. Train your students to be acute observers and elicit as many details as possible.

- ◆ Show the entire film without sound and have students make inferences. If you do this, present the topic and some key terms to the students prior to the showing.

- ◆ Present a topic to the students. Have the students generate questions about the topic and then use the selected nonprint media to answer, or begin to answer, the questions.

- ◆ Give the students key vocabulary or terms and use the nonprint media to define or categorize the concepts.

- ◆ Use two different types of nonprint media to teach a certain concept. Compare and contrast the presentation of the material in each.

These examples are only a few to spark your own creativity. Use the objectives of your lesson and your own ideas to shape the visual media you have available to you. As you can see, restructuring audiovisual material often requires that you actively preview it. By *actively preview*, we mean that during the first viewing, you are thinking of questions you need to ask and also possible student responses.

Besides the traditional audiovisual materials accessible through your district and state, other sources should not be overlooked. For example, personal slides can be used. Commercial videotapes can be shown for educational purposes (for example, we show parts of *A Man Called Horse* every year in our culture unit). Local museums and libraries have useful resources. Some television shows provide another source; get in the habit of reading your television guide on Sunday to see what is available during the week. Also, public radio often has good programs that can be shared with students.

Middle-School Lesson: Restructuring Textbook Material

Topic: Viruses, Bacteria, and Protista

Background: The topic is a chapter in the eighth-grade textbook *Life Science*, published by Silver Burdett. The students are taking an eighth-grade life-science class. The chapter is part of the animals and plants unit. The viruses, bacteria, and protista chapter is fifteen pages long and covers basic information about the simple organisms. In the middle of the chapter is a science experiment in which students can observe a paramecium; at the end of the chapter is a set of review questions. The lesson we propose would cover two periods; you will find that it is extremely difficult to design thinking lessons that can be completed in one period! The lesson based on this chapter is included in the sample lesson on page 56.

Notice how this lesson encourages students to learn the material in the textbook but requires them to think while doing so. The structure of the lesson also involves students in cooperative learning groups; such groupings complement complex-level thinking exercises nicely. Of course, doing simple experiments would be a natural extension of the lesson we have presented here. However, it was our intent to show how a complex-level thinking lesson could occur simply using the text, if no other resources were available.

The lesson illustrates how science is also a rich content area for complex-level thinking. Although many science textbooks lack complex-level lessons, materials are available to extend your use of the text.[4]

Although some textbooks are beginning to incorporate complex-level thinking lessons, most are low-level, basic texts, requiring little complex thinking.[5] Until textbook publishers begin to catch up with the demand for more thinking skills, the burden to restructure the material is on the teacher. Here are some examples of how you can restructure your textbooks:

✦ Check in the teacher's edition. Newest additions usually incorporate critical thinking. Look for what the authors believe are the complex-level thinking activities they have included. Decide if the activities/questions fit your criteria. There's no reason to redesign the wheel if the work has already been done for you!

✦ In a literature textbook, assign only the first two or three pages of the material to read. Students must write their own ending.

✦ In a literature textbook, have students make a matrix and compare several of the main characters for personal interests, humor, ability in school, relationship to parents, popularity, talent, kindness, and so on.

RESTRUCTURING: A textbook

Eighth-Grade Science Lesson, Chapter 16, Virus, Bacteria, and Protista

State that a thinking lesson will occur:

"We are going to take a thoughtful approach to chapter 16. We will work on it for two days. I will practice asking types of follow-up questions, and I would like you to give reasons for your answers. I am going to ask you to analyze the content of the chapter."

Encounter the problem with the students.

Give students the handout *You Have Just Been Discovered by Science!* Ask them to choose a life form from the board. (Written on the board are AIDS virus, tuberculosis, blue-green algae, red algae, etc.) Students review sheet with the teacher.

Establish a common knowledge base.

Students read the chapter, paying particular attention to their chosen life form and its relationship to the others described.

HOMEWORK: Students write descriptive answers to the four questions on the handout. Students are encouraged to use as much descriptive vocabulary as possible.

Engage in the thinking task.

Second period: Review task. Assign students to cooperative learning groups by topics (i.e., each group has a representative from each life form). Using their collective knowledge (no texts open), they categorize vocabulary from the chapter into the three categories: virus, bacteria, protista. Each student fills out sheet with input from everyone. Last fifteen minutes texts can be open.

Discuss the insights and results.

"Which vocabulary fits in two categories? Which vocabulary fits in all categories?"

Students can do question 3 on page 289: *"Do you think that viruses are alive? Give at least one reason for your answer."*

Classify the vocabulary on the board into these categories:

VIRUS	BACTERIA	PROTISTA

YOU HAVE JUST BEEN DISCOVERED BY SCIENCE!

1. Where were you found?

2. How are you like other simple life?

3. How are you different?

4. How do you affect other kinds of life?

From *Life Science* (Morristown, N.J.: Silver Burdett Co., 1982).

- ✦ Use only the pictures, tables, or graphs in the textbook for discussion or inference activities. Teach the students how to survey only the pictures and the main headings as a method to gather information.
- ✦ Have the students read only the questions at the end of the selection or have them read the questions prior to reading.
- ✦ Bring to class two different textbooks on the same topic and at the same grade level and have students critically analyze the contents in both.
- ✦ With science textbooks, use the experiments within the chapter to generate parallel experiments. Or, copy all chapter vocabulary on the board. Ask students to classify the words into as few groups as possible. Use a standard dictionary or text glossary to help.

As in the previous section, these are only selected examples to spark your own ideas. Textbooks are used frequently in the classrooms, so when restructuring you must look at the material in a new way. Meet with colleagues at the same grade level to brainstorm possible ideas.

We would like to leave this section on textbooks with one note of caution. Restructuring material should not circumvent the use of the material by the student. In other words, teaching thinking should not make the textbook irrelevant. At times, students must interact with textbooks on a one-to-one basis. We need only to see declining SAT scores to realize that students must learn how to approach a piece of written material and think critically about it.

High-School Lesson: Restructuring Trade Books [6]

Topic: Acquiring Knowledge

Background: This high-school lesson is part of a unit on the overall question, How do people acquire knowledge? This lesson comes toward the end of the unit. Students begin the unit by doing a prewriting activity about any experience from which they learned something. Then, students explore different ways knowledge is acquired by reading a number of books, including *Flowers for Algernon, By the Waters of Babylon,* and Plato's *Allegory of the Den.* The final book the students read is *Walkabout* by James Vance Marshall.

Two children, a thirteen-year-old girl and her eight-year-old brother, find themselves left to survive in the Australian outback after their plane crashes, four hundred miles from its destination. The children, reared in the tradition of the Charleston South, find their only companion and guide is a young aborigine bushboy who is fulfilling the rite of manhood for his tribe—the walkabout. Several themes course through the book—cultural contrasts, survival, fear, tradition, prejudice, sex roles, and more.

This lesson, based on the material in *Walkabout,* is outlined on page 58.

RESTRUCTURING: Tradebooks

High-School Literature Lesson:
Walkabout by James Vance Marshall

State that a thinking lesson will occur:

"I will be asking focusing questions during small-group thinking task stage and during the insights and results stage (teacher strategy). *You will be expected to participate, using precise and specific words* (student behavior). *You will be identifying broad concepts and making generalizations* (student behavior). *You will turn in writing on the identified concepts and how they are learned/demonstrated in each culture* (student behavior)."

Encounter the problem with the students.

"Your task today will be to identify the concepts in Walkabout *and to describe how these concepts are demonstrated in the contrasting cultures."*

Establish a common knowledge base.

1. All students have read the book.
2. Review how to form concepts and make generalizations.
3. Review past ideas of how knowledge is gained.
4. Define the contrasting cultures.

Engage in the thinking task.

Brainstorming: In small groups, students participate in the brainstorming process to produce at least three and no more than five concepts covered by the book (death, prejudice, survival, sex roles, tradition, religion, etc.).

Writing: Each student then fills out a sheet (see sample worksheet) describing those concepts as they are played out by each culture/character in the story.

Sample Worksheet

Discuss the insights and results.

Groups can be formed by concept or total group discussion can occur by concept. *"How does each student see the cultural contrast? Are there any concepts that are expressed universally between the cultures?"*

C O N C E P T S	Aborigine Australia	South Carolina United States

Students write their chosen concepts/categories

Trade books (the term we use to describe materials such as fiction, nonfiction, magazines, and newspapers) can be highly motivating for students as they are a welcome change from the textbook format. The literature-based approach to reading and the Great Books series are both examples of how complex-level thinking can be infused into the language-arts curriculum.* School and public libraries are excellent resources, as are your own subscriptions and those of your friends. Use these materials in a number of different ways:

✦ Trade books can be compared for similarities and differences. For example, with fiction materials, read several books by the same author for compare-and-contrast activities. You can also use foreign magazines on the same topic for comparison purposes.

✦ Use only the pictures in magazines. Do not allow the students to read the text. Use the pictures as the focus of your discussion or activity.

✦ Use newspapers to discuss language use, particularly in displaying biases or clichés.

✦ You can collect fiction books that fall into the same category (e.g., survival, science, fiction, mystery, humor) and look for patterns. Then, analyze the material according to the pattern.

✦ With biographies, a number of possibilities exist. For example, students can compare two different biographies for differences or compare an autobiography with a biography.

Relating Individual Lessons to Each Other

The three examples cited above are individual lessons. However, as you can see from reading the examples, a good thinking lesson builds upon others before it and suggests future lessons as well. You cannot teach discrete thinking lessons very easily if you are using the conceptual-infusion approach to thinking. Therefore, lessons can (and need to) be related to each other in a number of ways. First, you can develop the same thinking skill and/or concept across discipline areas over a period of time. For example, you might have the concept of *change* in your classroom, and every thinking lesson you do relates to this theme.

Lessons also can be integrated through the use of units, either teacher-developed or commercially acquired. A unit is a series of lessons, similar to the ones we have listed above, that fit together in a logical sequence. For example, the first lesson could be an introductory lesson to a unit on the Middle East.

---

*The only curriculum area we have not illustrated with a sample lesson is math; however, math, like all the other curriculum areas, is full of opportunities for complex-level thinking. At the elementary or junior-high level, we recommend any of Marilyn Burns's materials.

Units provide the teacher with the opportunity to develop thinking skills and concepts over a long period within a certain theme or topic. Interdisciplinary units are best, because of their conceptual, broad focus. Anne Udall and Shirley Schiever developed a list of questions you need to answer satisfactorily when designing an interdisciplinary unit of study: [7]

+ Is your unit theme related to the district curriculum?

+ Does your unit have a broad theme?

+ Is your unit interdisciplinary?

+ Does your unit have clearly stated goals and objectives for content, thinking processes, and products?

+ Does your unit have a number of comprehensive activities that develop your goals and objectives?

+ Does your unit have provisions for a variety of learning styles?

+ Does your unit have activities that progress sequentially and logically?

+ Does your unit include ways to evaluate your content, process, and products?

Developing units takes time and energy, but having your own material can be well worth the effort. Publishing companies also produce already designed units or individual learning packets that can be used with little adaptation. For example, Zephyr Press, our publisher, has a number of learning packets for students that encourage complex-level thinking. Another useful resource is a book by Edith Doherty and Louise Evans on how to develop your own curriculum units.[8] Simulation games can also be used as a catalyst for a series of related thinking lessons.[9]

The eventual goal is the development of a thinking curriculum for your classroom. If such a curriculum is already in place in your district or school, then you are lucky. Otherwise, the creation of a thinking curriculum will take place over time, with trial and error. As you become more familiar with the techniques of teaching thinking and develop more lessons, an encompassing structure will emerge. Resources are available as well to begin the process of developing a thinking curriculum.[10]

Conclusion

In this chapter, you have begun the journey toward creating the thoughtful classroom. Going beyond isolated thinking lessons and infusing your classroom with interrelated, conceptually designed lessons are huge steps on the journey. However, the greatest hurdle is yet to come: How do you become a successful tour guide as you teach the lessons you have developed? In the next chapter, we will answer that question.

6

Tour Guide Job Description: Nine Teacher Strategies in the Thoughtful Classroom

If you make people think they are thinking, they will love you.
If you really make them think, they will hate you.

Don Marquis, *The Sun Dial*

If thinking is not a spectator sport, then teaching thinking is surely hard work—in other words, teaching thinking is not for the fainthearted! The importance of the teacher in teaching thinking cannot be overlooked. We can teach any number of thinking processes using any number of programs or materials in any content area or subject. Yet how the teacher teaches is the important part. The teacher sets the tone and direction of any thinking activity. We can have the best lesson in the world—solid content information, a relevant topic, and a well-prepared discussion—but it is the time in the classroom that "makes or breaks" the success of the lesson.

A thinking lesson is orchestrated primarily through the strategies the teacher demonstrates. So, what strategies do teachers need to exhibit when teaching thinking? We will highlight nine strategies that we believe are critical to the success of any thinking lesson. Undoubtedly, more strategies could be added to the list, but our experience and research have shown these nine to be important:[1]

1. The teacher will focus and refocus students on task.
2. The teacher will ask open-ended questions.
3. The teacher will ask extension questions.
4. The teacher will wait for student responses.
5. The teacher will accept a variety of student responses.
6. The teacher will encourage student interaction.
7. The teacher will not give opinions or value judgments.
8. The teacher will not repeat student responses.
9. The teacher will ask students to reflect on their thinking.

These teaching strategies and how to develop them are the focus of this chapter. In the next section, each strategy will be discussed using the following format:

+ the strategy will be defined,
+ two scenarios illustrating a nonthoughtful and a thoughtful classroom will be presented to spark recollections about your own experiences,
+ ways to develop the teacher strategy will be explained, and
+ problems you might encounter when using the strategy will be identified.

At the end of the chapter, we make suggestions for implementing the teacher strategies.

The first three teacher strategies we discuss are directly concerned with specific questioning skills. Teachers ask as many as three hundred to four hundred questions a day, for a variety of purposes.[2] Because teachers use questions frequently to promote thinking, considerable attention has been given to the art of questioning when teaching complex-level thinking. Questioning behavior includes a wide range of strategies and techniques.

Teacher Strategy #1:
The Teacher Will Focus and Refocus Students on Task

Definition: The teacher makes sure that students are staying on the topic of discussion or that written work is consistent with the assigned task. If students stray from the topic, the teacher brings students back to the discussion topic or the focus of the written work.

The teacher will focus and . . .

. . . refocus students on task.

Scenario #1

NONTHOUGHTFUL CLASSROOM	THOUGHTFUL CLASSROOM
Mrs. Harrison is approaching the end of a unit on prejudice and stereotyping. The students have been reading a number of sources and completing activities. It is time to have a summary discussion. She is very busy—the school play is next week and the end of the quarter is around the corner, so she jots down some questions for discussion during her lunch hour. As the students enter the classroom, Mrs. Harrison begins the discussion. She finds herself asking a series of questions very quickly, one right after another, and notices that her students quickly lose interest in her original questions. The students stray from the topic and Mrs. Harrison is unable to bring them back to the original discussion. In fact, she is a bit confused about her original objective and ends the discussion, feeling discouraged and angry.	Mrs. Harrison has just finished reading this book and would like to try some of our recommended techniques. She is approaching the end of a unit on prejudice and stereotyping. The students have been reading a number of sources and completing activities. It is time to have a summary discussion. She is very busy, but somehow she finds the time to sit down with the librarian after school and pinpoint the focus of her discussion. She jots down some questions for discussion and then spends some time contemplating possible student responses. At dinner that night, Mrs. Harrison tries some of her questions out on her daughter and husband, who are more than willing to argue with her! Satisfied, the next day she begins the discussion by writing one question on the board exactly as she had worded it the day before. Then, she states the question clearly to the class. She soon finds her students to be engaged in a lively debate. When the students begin to stray and discuss other, unrelated aspects of the book, Mrs. Harrison points out the focusing question on the board. The other question she wrote down is not used.

These two scenarios highlight the importance of keeping students focused on the task.* Directing the students' attention is a preliminary step to achieving complex-level thinking. If students (and the teacher) are distracted and stray off the topic, little productive, meaningful thinking will take place. The teacher's role, then, is to make sure that students stay on task during a complex-level thinking lesson, whether it's during a discussion or with a written assignment.

---

*The scenarios we use in this chapter are slightly exaggerated versions of some of our own experiences in the classroom. We use the same situation in paired scenarios to show how the outcomes might differ if some of the strategies we propose are used in the thoughtful classroom.

How can you begin to focus students on task? Perhaps the key technique you can use is to prepare discussion or activity questions beforehand. This piece of advice is the most important one we will give about the teaching of thinking. If questions are prepared prior to the discussion, focusing students will not be a problem. Although Mrs. Harrison wrote down questions beforehand in both scenarios, notice the difference in the time and attention she gave this task in the two scenes. It will be necessary to find time to do this type of preparation, but the effort will be well rewarded. The Great Books Foundation suggests that one well-thought-out question can keep a group of students going for over an hour.[3] The task, then, in preparing questions before teaching is to generate one to four questions that will sustain an hour-long discussion. The following techniques and suggestions will assist you in learning to prepare questions:

1—Write down the objectives of the lesson.

What do you want students to learn? Every lesson has a multitude of directions it can go. For example, when discussing famous Black Americans, should students learn about discrimination and racism, or the parallels between famous Blacks and famous whites? Decide what knowledge or processes you want students to use and/or gain from the lesson. (Writing down objectives does not exclude the "teachable moment" that often happens during complex-level thinking lessons, when students and the teacher discover unplanned but very important generalizations. However, it does help prevent the numerous "unteachable moments" that can happen when objectives are NOT written down. We refer you to a wonderful chapter in a book by Elliot Eisner on the usefulness and uselessness of objectives.[4])

2—Write down the discussion questions.

Have one main question that is well phrased and clear. Have several follow-up questions to use if the first question doesn't succeed. Keep the written questions near you during the discussion or activity—they are not useful left on your desk at home!

3—Use your colleagues as sounding boards.

Your friends and professional contacts can help form good questions. Tell them the material you are using and the objectives you want to reach and then brainstorm possible questions for use.

4—Use a cognitive map a few times a year.

Hilda Taba was one of the first people to advocate the use of cognitive maps, which can be excellent tools when learning how to teach thinking. An example of a cognitive map, adapted from one proposed by Hilda Taba, is presented below.

Sample Cognitive Map

BACKGROUND: Students were preparing research papers about a famous person in history and were required to write a final chapter about his or her possible impact on history. This was a difficult task for many of them. This lesson was designed to show students one way they could think about someone's impact on history. After the lesson, the students could apply this strategy to their own subject.

LESSON: Students were shown a film about Amelia Earhart. Then students were asked to name some things that she is remembered for. Next, students were asked to name some possible effects of her accomplishments. Finally, students were asked to think about possible consequences of these effects. In the columns are possible student answers to the three questions.

First Question: What are the accomplishments Amelia Earhart will be remembered for?	Second Question: What are some changes that might occur as a result of her accomplishments?	Third Question: What are some further changes that might happen as a result of these changes?
First woman to solo across Atlantic.	became famous more women wanted to try	wanted more attention got more money backlash from men
First woman to fly intercontinental solo.	women wanted to fly in service people began to accept idea of women pilots wanted to break other records	military considered women pilots women became more militant women entered into other areas higher self-esteem tried other things
First woman to attempt flight around the world.	shock/sadness fear of flying increased men began to say women could not do same things better safety equipment was developed other people wanted to break record	denial of her death few pilots more business for psychiatrists women less likely to be accepted planes to do more more money invested record broken quickly

This cognitive map was adapted from the cognitive maps suggested in the Taba Teaching Strategy manuals. See Institute for Staff Development, eds., 1971. *Hilda Taba Teaching Strategies Program: Units 1,2,3,4.* Miami, Fla.: Author.

As you can see from the example, in a cognitive map you write out not only the questions you want to ask, but also all the responses you can think of that students might have. Like writing your objectives down, this activity forces you to think through the discussion and map out the possible directions it might go. Using this method, decisions can also be made about the best question(s) to use.[5]

There are many different types of cognitive maps; we will discuss others in detail in chapter 7 (when discussing their use with students). We are not advocating the use of cognitive maps for every lesson; the time demand is too much. Yet we do suggest that you try mapping a lesson at least once or twice; the insights you gain from the activity will be invaluable.

5—Write the main question or questions on the board so students may see the question.

Most of us (more than eighty percent) are visual learners.[6] However, discussions (a large part of teaching thinking for most of us) are mainly auditory. Writing the question where everyone can see it will keep the focus on the topic. If the teacher or the students stray, the question on the board serves as a reminder.

6—Have an activity or series of activities that will allow you to evaluate student progress.

Students are more likely to keep focused if they know that they are expected to write a summary or complete an activity for evaluation. Types of activities can include:

+ writing down a response to a question prior to discussion,

+ writing down a summary of the discussion after talking, and

+ telling students they will get credit for contributing to the discussion (more on this later).

7—Make sure any focusing questions have the characteristics recommended by the Great Books Foundation.

These are as follows:

+ the teacher writes clear and specific questions,

+ the teacher has genuine doubt about the answer or answers to the questions, and

+ the teacher cares about the questions.

8—Use tape recorders or video equipment to assess
the questions in the lesson.*

As you listen to or view the tape, write down your questions. Analyze them
for their ability to keep students focused. Do not evaluate the entire lesson!
The danger of using audio equipment is that we tend to judge ourselves too
harshly. Focus on specific information you can gain from the tapes.

Problems You Might Encounter

The biggest problem is not letting students discuss irrelevant material.
Students love discussions, but many of them have had little practice in
staying on task. Many of the suggestions above will help with this problem.
Another problem will occur when the discussion goes in an unplanned
direction, requiring you to think on your feet. Our experience has taught us
that, with practice, we learned how to "milk" a discussion when this
occurred. The challenge and fun of teaching thinking is that it is impossible
to plan for every contingency.

Teacher Strategy #2:
The Teacher Will Ask Open-ended Questions

Definition: The teacher asks questions that have more than one answer or
questions that cannot be answered yes or no.

Scenario #2

NONTHOUGHTFUL CLASSROOM	THOUGHTFUL CLASSROOM
Ms. Ladd has a weekly class meeting, and lately she has been using that time to involve the students in complex-level thinking around affective issues. Ms. Ladd wants to discuss the playground behavior at their school because more and more conflicts are being reported. She assembles the students in a circle and begins to ask some questions: Is it okay for kids to fight on the playground? Was John right when he hit Henry back after Henry hit him? Ms. Ladd does not notice that most of the student responses are short, and that she is doing most of the talking.	Mrs. Mina is a colleague of Ms. Ladd, and when she heard about the discussion topic, she decided to determine her students' thinking on the topic. She gathered her students together in a similar way, and began the discussion. She asked the students some questions: What are some of the problems on the playground? Why do students fight? What are some of the solutions? When two students are fighting, what can you do to stop the fight? The students, along with Mrs. Mina, begin to gain valuable insights into playground dynamics.

---

*In chapters 6 and 7, we mention evaluation tools; chapter 8 discusses specific evaluation methods in detail.

The teacher will ask
open-ended questions.

Open-ended questions are the best questions to ask when conducting a complex-level thinking activity or discussion. Open-ended questions are the opposite of closed questions. Closed questions tend to be associated with the lower levels of thinking, such as memory and recall. Here are some examples of closed questions:

✦ In what year was Nicolas Ceausescu executed in Romania?

✦ What months are named after people? (Hint: there are three and the answer can be found in your nearest Trivial Pursuit® box.)

✦ What chemical element has the atomic number of thirty-six?

We demand less of ourselves mentally when we are asked a closed question. You can test this statement by asking yourself any of the closed questions above and observing your mental activity. You will notice a lack of cognitive exertion. Students in your classroom have the same experience when they are asked a low-level question.

In contrast, open-ended questions have more than one response. There are no right answers to open-ended questions. When asked this type of question, an individual must ponder an answer before responding. These are some examples of open-ended questions:

✦ Discuss the differences between the revolutions in Eastern Europe in the 1980s and the French Revolution in 1798.

✦ Was President Bush right in sending troops to Panama in late 1989 to overthrow the government of General Noriega?

✦ How might this experiment be designed differently to study another variable?

Open-ended questions force students to think in a more expanded and thoughtful way. You can again observe your mental activity by having someone ask you an open question from the examples above and watching your mental response. You will notice the mental effort required by the question.

Some important lessons on questioning can be learned by taking a moment to study the first two questions. The first one is an implied question—although it is not in question form, you are posing a problem. Sometimes we ask questions similar to this example, but we may not recognize that we are, in fact, asking an open-ended question. The art of asking questions that are not questions is a good technique to develop—see Dillon for a more detailed discussion on teaching and the art of questioning.[7]

The second question implies an open-ended question because of the nature of the content. In other words, this question cannot easily be answered with a yes or no even though the wording is closed. The phrasing of the question is also slanted and indicates that the person asking the question has a particular bias. This is a common mistake many of us make—we ask a thought-provoking question in a closed manner, thereby inadvertently shutting down thinking and indicating our prejudices. Think for a moment how you might ask this question differently.

Time's up. How about: What is your opinion of President Bush's decision to send troops to Panama to overthrow the government of General Noriega? This wording does not influence the person who hears the question and allows the person to think nonjudgmentally about the material.

The first scenario in this section has some examples of closed questions that could easily be changed to open questions. Try to reword those questions so they are more open.

Ways to Develop Teacher Strategy #2

Like all the teacher strategies, developing open-ended questions takes practice. Many of the earlier suggestions for keeping students on task apply here:

1—Write questions down before the lesson and have them where they can be seen at all times during the lesson.

You can write the question on the board so your students can see it as well. Perhaps emphasize the first word or words of the question to indicate the openness of the inquiry.

2—Have a discussion with your students specifically about open-ended questions.

Define what they are and why they are important. You will be surprised how quickly students understand the difference between the types of questions. Once you have explained this teacher strategy to the students, give them opportunities to "catch you" asking yes or no questions. In one class, students earned points for recognizing closed questions the teacher asked. This exercise will also improve student listening.

3—Use a tape recorder to assess your questions.

As in strategy #1, this exercise provides you with an opportunity to assess your progress.

4—Listen to other people asking questions and practice rewording their questions in a more open matter.

The next time you are at a faculty meeting or an educational conference, listen to the presenters. You will begin to notice how frequently people ask closed questions and how this action shuts down the cognitive process.

Problems You Might Encounter

The biggest problem will be your desire to ask spontaneous questions. When a student sparks our thinking, the tendency is to ask a question that is not part of our lesson plan. That is not all bad. However, when you are first learning how to teach thinking, such an action can be disastrous. Once started, we quickly return to our old, familiar patterns and begin to ask closed questions. The result is a slowing down of complex thinking. Avoid the urge to ask unprepared questions at first!

A second problem will be the tendency to ask a great open-ended question and immediately follow up with a similar, related question, with slightly different wording. An example: "What were some of the concerns the shipwrecked men had on the first day? How do you think they felt?" Our intent by asking the second question is to clarify for the students; what we do is only confuse. It is important to ask the original question as planned and allow the students an opportunity to consider their answers. Extension questions should be used only if necessary. Some ways to do this effectively are covered in the next section.

Teacher Strategy #3:
The Teacher Will Ask Extension Questions

Definition: Teacher asks students for further information about their answers. Students can be asked to clarify, support, or elaborate on an earlier response.

Scenario #3

NONTHOUGHTFUL CLASSROOM	THOUGHTFUL CLASSROOM
Mr. Hernandez is discussing a problem-solving math activity. His students are in cooperative learning groups. He asks from each group the answer to the problem. The "reporter" in each group responds with their answer. After the answers are written on the chalkboard, students are asked to look for agreement among the groups. Mr. Hernandez then tells the students the correct answer and demonstrates a problem-solving technique. When he is finished, the students are given a new problem to solve.	Mr. Hernandez is discussing a problem-solving math activity. His students are in cooperative learning groups. The students have just finished solving the problem and are reporting their answers. After each group responds, Mr. Hernandez asks for one student in the group to explain their process for solving the problem. If necessary, the students are encouraged to go to the chalkboard and diagram their thinking. Mr. Hernandez frequently pursues answers from students with follow-up questions such as "What is your reasoning?" or "How did you decide that?" When one student says, "We took it and added it to the other stuff," Mr. Hernandez stops the description and asks for definitions of "it" and "stuff." The students begin to glean a better understanding of effective problem-solving techniques.

Asking extension questions is a key teacher strategy. Students are conditioned to give answers quickly, without much thought; therefore, the follow-up questions that are asked can be crucial to sparking complex-level thinking. There are three main types of extension questions: clarification, support, and elaboration.

Clarification questions provide you and the students with valuable information. Students may give an initial answer that appears to be clear and concise. However, a follow-up question may reveal that the answer lacks logic or consistency. Clarification questions are most often used for explaining vague vocabulary. In the Taba teaching strategies manuals,[8] a wonderful illustration is reported: A teacher was observing her young students classifying rocks. She watched one boy who was placing rocks into categories that indicated some understanding of geology. She asked him to explain his classification system. The boy responded: "By age." The teacher was impressed by his grasp of geology and out of curiosity followed up with the question: "What do you mean by age?" The boy said: "Big rocks and little rocks."

The two other types of extension questions, support and elaboration, probe student reasoning. Support questions are those designed to elicit the student's reasoning. An answer may be clearly stated, and yet you wish to probe for the thinking behind it. Elaboration questions are similar to support questions; however, in these instances, students are asked to embellish on their initial answer, with more detail or ideas. Unlike clarification questions, these types of questions are more likely to require complex thinking.

Ways to Develop Teacher Strategy #3

Developing this strategy requires that you listen to your students' responses carefully and ask extension questions when necessary. This strategy is more difficult to develop than the earlier ones. Here are some helpful hints for asking extension questions:

1—Be vigilant about listening for answers that appear vague or unclear.

Students are very adept at giving quick responses and will frequently use nebulous terms such as "stuff" or "thing." Set the expectation that they should be concise with language by asking them to define or explain their terminology.

2—Write down a variety of extension questions and use them with students.

Here are some examples of clarification, support, and elaboration questions.

Clarification Questions:

What do you mean by _____?

Please say that in other words.

I am unclear about your meaning of_____.

Explain what you mean when you say _____.

How would you explain in your own words what Tom said?

What is a different way of saying that?

Support Questions:

Why?

What is your reasoning?

What is your strategy?

How did you decide?

Why does that make sense?

What evidence do you have?

What did we talk about that led you to that conclusion?

Where in our text is information to back up your assertion?

Elaboration Questions:

How is it like _____?

What will happen if _____?

What is missing?

Tell me more.

What would be an example?

Richard Paul and his fellow authors have developed a comprehensive list of questions in their critical thinking handbook.[9] They encourage teachers to use these questions when employing the Socratic method of questioning.* Although they have classified their questions differently from ours, their list is very helpful and has been included in appendix B.

Problems You Might Encounter

We have noticed three main problems when developing this strategy. First, students are surprised (sometimes astounded!) when asked to extend their thinking. You will notice blank stares and hear "I don't know." Do not accept "I don't know." If you do, students will quickly learn they need not push their thinking. Follow an "I don't know" statement with one of several responses we mentioned earlier:

◆ "Ask me a question that would help you understand."

◆ "If you did know, what would you say?"

◆ "Pretend you do know and make something up."

◆ "I don't know only means you need more time to think—listen to others and I'll come back to you" (then make sure you do).

You can also ask other students to help the student with his or her reasoning.

---

*The Socratic method of questioning is simple to describe but difficult to use: while engaging in discourse with students, the teacher uses probing and clarifying questions to guide student thinking and elicit complex understanding of a topic.

The second major problem will be time, THE precious commodity of teachers teaching thinking. When you begin to ask for reasons and support in a discussion, time is needed. (One colleague of ours remarked after watching one of us teach: "If I taught that way, I would never get anything done!") It is difficult, if not impossible, to ask follow-up questions of every student. As you develop your skills, you will begin to ask selectively, calling on some key students to illustrate reasoning or clarification. Be wary of calling on the same students over and over.

A related issue will be restlessness from your students. Again, they will not be used to the pace of a thinking skills discussion. There will be restlessness and perhaps some perceived boredom. We have discovered that this is a difficult stage to move through. Do not let the class mood dictate your pace. Explain to the students what you are doing and why. If you role-model this strategy and allow students to practice it over time, they should begin to adjust to the pace and enjoy the opportunity to think. You must model the enjoyment and enthusiasm, however; if you are bored, your students will be too.

One final problem may be students' lack of vocabulary. Many extension questions are highly dependent upon sufficient vocabulary. Be on the lookout for opportunities to develop student vocabulary, either during the lesson or as a later activity. (As an aside: all thinking is related to vocabulary, so this suggestion is applicable regardless of the strategy you are practicing.)

These first three strategies only begin to cover the complex art of asking questions when conducting thinking activities. A number of other intricate issues are apparent. For example, matching the type of question to the thinking lesson you are teaching is very important (e.g., a problem-solving lesson requires different types of questions from a critical-thinking lesson). The problem of when to ask and when not to ask questions arises frequently. As you become more aware of the importance of questions, refining your questioning behavior will be a natural goal. A number of resources are available to help you with your questioning strategy.[10]

Teacher Strategy #4:
The Teacher Will Wait for Student Responses

Definition: The teacher waits for more than five seconds for a student to respond to a question.

Scenario #4

NONTHOUGHTFUL CLASSROOM	THOUGHTFUL CLASSROOM
Mr. Harland is beginning a discussion on the book *Stone Fox.* He has finished reading the book to the students and is very moved by the ending. He wonders if the students related to the plight of the boy. In fact, he wrote down several good, open-ended questions the night before. He pauses and says to the students: "How did the outcome of the race affect the boy and his grandfather?" Immediately he calls on Maria, the girl who always has a "good" answer to any question. She gives an interesting reply and he looks for other raised hands. Quickly, he calls on Jermaine, another verbal student in his class. When Jermaine is finished he looks around for more student hands. Several seconds later, discouraged and upset because no hands are raised, he says in exasperation: "Well, I guess you don't have any feelings about this book. Let's go on to math."	Mr. Harland is beginning a discussion on the book *Stone Fox.* He has finished reading the book to the students and is very moved by the ending. He wonders if the students related to the plight of the boy. In fact, he wrote down several good, open-ended questions the night before. He pauses and says to the students: "How did the outcome of the race affect the boy and his grandfather?" The teacher waits calmly, watching his students' faces for signs of understanding, while counting to ten to himself. He sees Maria's hand go up quickly but resists the urge to call on her immediately. Slowly, other hands are tentatively raised. When there are at least six hands up, he calls on one student and then another. Soon, a lively discussion has begun.

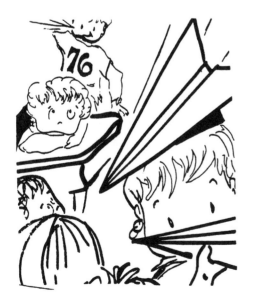

The teacher will wait—but not too long.

Wait time is a strategy used primarily in complex-thinking discussions and is less crucial in writing or reading activities. The average teacher waits one second.[11] Take a second (!) to really experience how short a time one second is. Minimum wait time should be five seconds, and we highly recommend a wait time of at least ten seconds.

The two different scenarios illustrate the significant role that wait time plays in a discussion. As illustrated in the nonthoughtful classroom, having little or no wait time benefits only those students who think quickly or have glib answers. Short wait time encourages answers with little depth. In the other scenario, you can see how appropriate wait time will lead to much greater participation by all students. A teacher who develops long wait time is telling his or her students that they have time to think and that all students will be included in the discussion.

Different types of wait time exist.[12] After an initial focusing question, the teacher waits for students to begin an answer. The second type of wait time occurs after students give the answer. How long do teachers wait for further explanation or elaboration by the same student OR by other students? This is the wait time we give students when we ask follow-up questions.

Teachers, as a group, intensely dislike silence within their classrooms. They feel that there may be nothing happening—the kids aren't *doing* anything! Stop reading RIGHT NOW and count ten seconds. Imagine that space of time with no noise in your classroom—just silence as you allow students the opportunity to think. For most of us ten seconds seems like forever! Mr. Harland's behavior is typical—teachers cover up their discomfort with any silence by using forced bravado and jokes, thereby disrupting any thinking that could be sparked by good questions.

Ways to Develop Teacher Strategy #4

Because of general teacher discomfort with silence, wait time is very difficult to develop. The only way to improve wait time is to practice doing it. A number of techniques can help:

1—Count to ten to yourself before calling on any student.

This forces you to concentrate on the time and will lessen your anxiety.

2—Tell the students what wait time is, and why you are practicing developing it.

Students as young as third grade can grasp the concept of wait time and will support your efforts. In fact, it is helpful to tell impatient students that you are giving everyone time to think. Also, explain to students that people have different wait times. In short, use the term "wait time" frequently in your class.

3—Have students write down responses to a question before you call on anyone.

This activity, besides developing wait time, will allow less-verbal students an opportunity to participate.

4—Have students share their reactions to the questions with a partner or in a small group before participating in a large group.

This practice is similar to the one listed above.

**5—While you are waiting, demonstrate something or write
   your question on the board.**

In other words, keep busy! Doing something will keep you from worrying about whether anyone will respond.

**6—Wait until one-half to three-quarters of the students
   have their hands raised.**

You can tell the students that you are doing this to encourage wait time and to give everyone an opportunity to think.

7—Watch students' faces.

The looks on students' faces will tell you quickly if they understand the question. Frequently, students will even tell you that they don't understand.

8—Tell students NOT to raise their hands.

You will call on *anyone*. This puts responsibility on all to be ready. If you use wait time but still call on only the students who have their hands raised, the less active students will continue to not participate.

Problems You Might Encounter

Wait time really works! You will be amazed at how many students begin to participate when everyone is allowed the opportunity to think. Yet, you may encounter obstacles. One problem will be your discomfort about silence in your classroom. Notice your own awkwardness and need to fill the silence. Be aware of wanting to speak too soon and not giving wait time a chance.

We have also noticed that wait time can be sabotaged if you ask students to think about a question and then call on only students who have their hands raised. Students may learn that it is "safe" not to think as long as they don't put up their hands. Calling on all students will alleviate this problem.

Another common problem will occur when you ask a student a question but he or she doesn't respond. You wait ten seconds, then twenty or thirty more, maybe even as long as a minute. You realize that it is punishing to the student to continue to wait. If a student says "I don't know," you may respond with the suggestions we gave on page 73. If the student still doesn't say anything, rephrase the question so that the student can vocalize something. Sometimes this means asking a more basic thinking question.

The fourth major problem concerns adjusting to the need for different types of wait time. When you first practice wait time, it will be relatively easy to learn to wait for the first student response after the initial question. Trouble occurs with successive student responses and with secondary questions. Wait time is quickly forgotten as you begin to pick up the pace and call on people quickly. Be cautious about falling into this trap.

Rowe lists some other "mental hazards" that can interfere with wait-time results.[13] These include making vague commands like "think," repeating student responses (see teacher strategy #8), saying "isn't it?" and "right?" and using the phrase "don't you think that . . . ?" Minimize these verbal behaviors.

Teacher Strategy #5:
The Teacher Will Accept a Variety of Student Responses

Definition: The teacher asks more than one student for an answer to a question, making sure that as many students as possible have an opportunity to respond.

Scenario #5

NONTHOUGHTFUL CLASSROOM	THOUGHTFUL CLASSROOM
Miss Jonston is conducting a discussion about the results from the class science project. She has prepared her questions and is aware of wait time. Her students are ready as Miss Jonston asks her first focusing question. She calls on Harry, and he responds. Tim then responds to the same question. The next question is asked, and a third student is called upon. Miss Jonston continues in this vein, asking a question and then having one, or maybe two, students answer, and then asking the next question. Miss Jonston is always a bit surprised at how quickly her discussions are finished, because everyone is always saying that complex-level thinking takes so much time!	Miss Jonston has seen the error of her ways and wants to try to conduct a discussion about the results from the class science project once more. As always, she has prepared her questions and is aware of wait time. Miss Jonston tells the students that she is going to work on wait time during the discussion, and asks them to write down their responses to her first question before raising their hands. After asking the first question, she calls on Jesus, then Phillip, and finally Sarah for her opinion. There are several other students who want to respond as well, so she calls on them. After hearing from a number of students in her class, Miss Jonston proceeds with the next question in her discussion. Each time a new point or question is raised, she solicits a wide range of responses. With these new techniques, even her quietest students venture opinions and ideas.

The teacher will accept a variety
of student responses.

Many teachers are in the habit of relying on a few students in their classrooms—the ones they know will have a thoughtful, interesting answer. Once we hear an answer that in our opinion is interesting, we move on to the next question. What frequently happens in this type of classroom is that students stop responding to questions. The less-verbal or slow students begin to instinctively count on the fact that the teacher is going to call on only a few students for responses. The quieter and/or less-motivated students relax and stop thinking.

Accepting a variety of answers means the teacher actively seeks a number of answers and withholds any overt approval or judgment (see strategy #7 for more on this aspect). When the teacher is able to accept different answers, larger numbers of students will participate. Consequently, more ideas will be received.

As more students are involved and motivated to share, the class as a whole will take greater responsibility for the discussion. Students will listen to each other more and spark each others' thinking, in turn increasing the likelihood of more complex thinking.

Ways to Develop Teacher Strategy #5

Some of the techniques we mentioned previously will also work with developing this strategy:

1—Keep a tally of student responses.

In one sixth-grade classroom, the teacher had students keep a tally sheet of which students contributed and how many times.

2—Tell students they must participate at least two times during a discussion or activity.

Give a grade or credit for participating.

3—Tell students that you are going to call on everyone, regardless of who raises his or her hand.

In fact, you can tell students not to raise their hands for certain questions and call on them at random.

4—Before calling on anyone, have students write down responses to the questions.

This technique is useful for this strategy because students have to demonstrate participation by writing; when you simply call on students without prior writing, some students will undoubtedly not participate.

5—Use cooperative learning techniques and a variety of groupings in your classroom when doing complex-level thinking activities.[14]

Different structures will meet the different learning styles of all your students, thereby encouraging wider participation.

6—Use specific questions to encourage variety.

Some questions are good for encouraging a number of different answers from students:

 ◆ What is a totally different answer?

 ◆ What is another solution?

 ◆ What are other alternatives?

 ◆ What are five different ways?

You will be able to think of similar types of questions with practice.

7—Reserve judgment when students respond.

This action will encourage other student answers. We will discuss this in more detail under teacher strategy #7.

8—Use cards with student names.

At the beginning of the year, make a deck of cards with all the students' names on them. Then, during the discussion or activity, call on students randomly using the cards. Explain to the students what you are doing before the lesson. Our experience has shown that students become involved in the lesson when the teacher uses this technique.[15]

Problems You Might Encounter

One possible major problem is a conditioned need to call on the same kids. Old habits die hard. We all know that certain students will provide us with "good" answers; these are the students we tend to recognize. When we first started teaching complex thinking and a lesson did not go well, our instinct was to call on the students who would rescue us. Patterns are particularly hard to break if you try to change behavior during the middle of the school year. The more practice you can have, the better the results will be.

Teacher Strategy #6:
The Teacher Will Encourage Student Interaction

Definition: The teacher encourages students to talk to each other, not strictly to her or him.

In teaching complex thinking, a primary goal is to develop more student interaction. Although little research exists to substantiate our belief that more student talk will lead to increased complex thinking, it makes sense that the less the teacher talks, the more opportunity students will have to interact and therefore empower each other's mental processes. Such an outcome is the whole focus of the journey you are on. Once students look to each other, the teacher is no longer the one with all the answers.

However, the typical classroom structure is centered around the teacher. Interaction among students occurs only with the teacher as the conduit. Look at the two classroom scenes presented in the previous scenario. Notice how in both, Miss Jonston asked a question and a student (or several) responded. Then, the teacher asked the next question. This pattern is common in many classrooms and will stifle complex thinking.

Here is how Miss Jonston might change her behavior to encourage student interaction:

Scenario #6

THOUGHTFUL CLASSROOM

Miss Jonston has seen the error of her ways and wants to try to conduct a discussion about the results from the class science project once more. As always, she has prepared her questions and is aware of wait time. Miss Jonston tells the students she is going to work on wait time during the discussion and asks them to write down their responses to her first question before raising their hands. After asking the first question, she calls on Jesus and then Phillip. She then asks Sarah her opinion of Phillip's ideas. There are several other students who want to respond as well, so she calls on them. Students are asked to talk to each other in pairs about the question. During the rest of the discussion, Miss Jonston continues to ask students to respond to each other.

The teacher will encourage
student interaction.

Getting students to talk to each other is only one part of student interaction. Their interactions must have depth and quality to them; otherwise, students are doing little more than socializing. One way to assure quality thinking is to develop questioning behavior by students. We have found this to be very difficult to do. Students can become proficient at answering complex-level questions from teachers, but to generate and ask their own questions is truly a challenge. Question asking by students can take years to develop; do not be discouraged if such student behavior does not show up quickly. We will discuss developing this behavior in more detail in chapter 7.

Ways to Develop Teacher Strategy #6

This strategy is closely related to accepting a variety of responses. Student interaction can be developed with a number of activities:

1—When one student says something, ask another student
   (or several) to respond to the presented statement.

For example, you can say: "Jeff, what do you think of Barbara's statement?"

2—Tell students you would like to hear them say "I agree with
   (student's name) because . . ." or "I disagree with
   (student's name) because . . .".

Keep a tally of the times students demonstrate this behavior and report it to the students.

3—When having a discussion, seat students in a circle so that
   they can see each other.

If you do nothing else, this simple technique will greatly improve student interaction. Students are forced to look at each other; distractions from sitting at desks are also minimized. Sit in the circle or walk around the outside, so that students are forced to look at each other. Do not stand while the students sit because such behavior only establishes you as the authority figure.

4—Reduce teacher talk to a minimum.

Do not give your opinion or judgment about the topic. Allow yourself only a certain number of questions or explanations.

5—Reinforce students when they respond to each other.

You can say such things as "Henry, it was great to hear you respond to Carol's ideas" or "Alberto, it is obvious you were really thinking about what Adam said."

6—Do regular exercises with your students that develop listening, trust, and discussion skills.

Part of getting students to interact is teaching them appropriate social skills. Some excellent resources listed in Notes can get you started.[16]

7—Use questions such as "Who will agree or disagree with Jeff?"

This type of question will encourage students to talk to each other.

8—Require students to paraphrase one another before contributing.

In order to give their ideas, students must summarize what the student before them said. This technique can be very successful in increasing listening skills.

9—Direct students to call upon one another.

For example, "Yolanda, please call on the next person."

Problems You Might Encounter

Increased student interaction will lead to greater student talk and higher motivation. Yet, encouraging student interaction is one of the most difficult teacher strategies to develop. As a result, students learn to not listen to each other; the teacher will tell all. Children have years of conditioning around the teacher as the authority, the focal point, the final say. They also have years of learning how to listen to the teacher and not to each other. Student opinions are often discounted by other students simply because they are made by students and not the teacher.

One major problem, then, may be our reluctance to let go of our control of the classroom. We are comfortable, unconsciously or not, with control-ling the action and tempo. It takes diligence and commitment to teach students to listen to and interact with each other. Students will want to look at you and talk to you. They will not trust the responses of other students. You need to "remove" yourself from the interactions as much as possible—let your students forget that you are there.

When you begin to remove yourself from the interactions, another problem you may encounter will be students' difficulty in focusing on each other in a serious manner. Students can become silly or inattentive when talking to a friend or boyfriend/girlfriend (in the older years). Again, students need continual practice and encouragement.

Teacher Strategy #7:
The Teacher Will Not Give Opinions or Value Judgments

Definition: The teacher does not give his or her opinion or tell students if their answers are good or bad.

Scenario #7

NONTHOUGHTFUL CLASSROOM	THOUGHTFUL CLASSROOM
Mr. Henry is working with his students on a class science-fair project. The class is meeting to discuss possible ideas for an experiment. It is a brainstorming session, and everyone has been asked to share ideas. The students have spent some time looking through library books about science experiments. Mr. Henry asks the opening question: "What might be some experiments we can do for our science project this year?" Students raise their hands and begin to respond. Mr. Henry writes the first few ideas on the board without much comment, until Matt, one of his bright students, gives an especially good idea. Mr. Henry exclaims "Great!" He continues to reinforce ideas that he likes with a "Good!" or "Great!" The discussion is over quickly.	Mr. Henry is working with his students on a class science-fair project. The class is meeting to discuss possible ideas for an experiment. It is a brainstorming session, and everyone has been asked to share ideas. The students have spent some time looking through library books about science experiments. Mr. Henry asks the opening question: "What might be some experiments we can do for our science project this year?" Students raise their hands and begin to respond. Mr. Henry records their answers on the board but gives little other verbal expression. Occasionally he will say "yes" or "uh-huh," and he nods his head a lot. One student asks him: "Was that a good answer?" and Mr. Henry asks him in return: "What do you think?"

Some teachers are shocked when we first suggest that they not give their opinions or value judgments. We hear: "But, but you have to let students know they are doing a good job . . . we have to reinforce them or they wouldn't give any answers." Yes, students have been trained to see the teacher as the person with the right or only answers, and this is one reason students neither support nor criticize each other. It is also the reason students continually ask teachers for reassurance and support that their ideas are good or "right."

Art Costa is a strong proponent of teaching without opinions, and he once demonstrated how the power of opinions can shut down thinking.[17] He began a mock discussion and solicited ideas from his adult audience. Several responses later, he said "good!" to an idea put forth. Within an instant, I could watch myself mentally shut down. I knew the person was "right" and had given the answer he was looking for, and I didn't need to think any longer. Your students will do the same thing (and do already, all the time) if you selectively comment on student responses.

If your students are going to think on complex levels, it is very important to break their "dependency habit." Teacher reinforcement is a powerful tool; it must be used very carefully when teaching complex thinking. Only then will students begin to listen to each other and depend on themselves.

Ways to Develop Teacher Strategy #7

This is a very difficult strategy to develop because of our own training to constantly reinforce students indiscriminately. Instead, during a thinking activity, you are training yourself to be an active listener to what the students are saying. When you are actively engaged in shared thinking with your students, there is no time for unconscious praise. Try some of these behaviors to help you when you find yourself reinforcing students:

1—Explain to your students why you are going to stop giving opinions.

Once again, students will surprise you with their awareness. Then, challenge your students to catch you at giving opinions or value judgments. Their astuteness will quickly train you.

2—Say something that is nonjudgmental after students talk.

Nonjudgmental statements include such phrases as "ok," "uh-huh," or "thank you."

3—Model nonverbal acceptance of all answers from students.

Nodding your head frequently and using eye contact both work. Accepting a student answer is different from telling a student his or her answer is right. This behavior is only to let students know they are being heard.

4—Keep yourself busy so that you don't have time to say "good."

For example, you can write responses on the board or overhead projector.

5—Tape yourself and count the number of times you
    give your opinion.

6—Acknowledge all students at the end of the discussion
    for the quality of their thinking.

Give your opinion or value judgment in a generalized way.

7—Hold your opinions until after the lesson.

If students ask you directly "What do you think?" turn the question around
and ask them "What do *you* think?" If you wish, after the lesson, you can
share your opinion, but make sure you preface your opinion with the
statement that you are only one voice.

8—Ask follow-up questions.

The Great Books Foundation states that one of the best ways you can
encourage students without judgment and show them that you are listening to what they say is through follow-up questions. In other words, a good
follow-up question is worth a thousand "Greats!" to a student.

Problems You Might Encounter

What do you do when a student gives a response that is clearly faulty in
reasoning and understanding? This is a difficult question and one of the
most common problems when developing this strategy. Try asking the
student some follow-up questions that will allow the student to see the lack
of reasoning. Avoid the urge to point out the mistake yourself. Another
solution we have found is to ask other students to analyze a student's
response. However, this suggestion should be tried only after your students have developed a safe, respectful environment. Students can often be
brutal without thinking. However, with practice, students will begin to do
what was previously your work. You can also use extension and clarification questions to expose a student's lack of logic.

What should you do in the opposite situation—when a student gives
an especially sharp answer or when a shy student speaks for the first time?
In the latter example, we have noticed that teachers like to give opinions
and value judgments when nonverbal or cognitively slower students begin
to talk in class. In either case, teachers ache to say "Great!" and often do.
Try to resist the urge! Talk to the student after class and praise him or her.
Build on the student's idea and encourage responses from other students.
This will reinforce the whole class.

Teacher Strategy #8:
The Teacher Will Not Repeat Student Responses

Definition: When a student gives a response, the teacher does not repeat what was just said but moves on to the next student or question.

Scenario #8

NONTHOUGHTFUL CLASSROOM	THOUGHTFUL CLASSROOM
Mrs. Locklee is conducting a discussion. Her questions are good, open-ended questions, and her students are having a lively discussion. Each time a student responds, Mrs. Locklee repeats the student answer. She asks Jerry to respond to Tim's answer, but he didn't hear Tim's response. She notices that her students don't seem to listen much to each other. The pattern in the classroom is that one student talks and then the teacher. Students do not interact very much with each other.	Mrs. Locklee is conducting a discussion. Her questions are good, open-ended questions, and her students are having a lively discussion. Each time a student responds, Mrs. Locklee is quiet. She encourages student interaction by asking the students to comment on each other's remarks; if students don't hear each other, they ask each other to repeat comments. Mrs. Locklee speaks rarely except to redirect the attention of her students or to ask a clarification question.

Teachers, on average, have been known to repeat student's responses thirty-one times in a twenty-minute lesson.[18] It is an unconscious habit most of us have developed in the classroom. Watch yourself for a day and notice how frequently you repeat student's responses. This "parroting behavior" potentially stifles complex thinking. Students do not listen to each other because they know the teacher will tell them everything that was said. Consequently, student-to-student interaction is shut down; the teacher is once again placed in the center of the discussion.

Ways to Develop Teacher Strategy #8

Our experience has been that teachers can train themselves to stop repeating student responses once they become aware of the habit. For most of us, it is simply an unconscious behavior. There are ways to become aware of repeating behaviors:

1—Use a tape recorder during a lesson to record yourself.

2—Use a peer coach—a colleague or friend who will
   write down behaviors you repeat.

This technique has worked very well with us. We will discuss some details on how to use a peer coach in chapter 8.

3—Ask your students to help you stop repeating.

4—Tell students to raise their hands if they cannot hear.

Watch for raised hands. If a response needs to be repeated, ask the student to do it.

5—Replace repeating behaviors with other verbal responses, such as "ok," "uh-huh," or "yes."

Make sure your responses are noncommittal and accepting but not judging.

Problems You Might Encounter

This strategy will begin to drop out once you develop some awareness. The major problem, then, is becoming aware. Once this occurs, you will find it easy to not repeat student responses. Remember that clarifying or rewording the student's response is a form of repeating. Continue to assess yourself on a regular basis—this behavior has a tendency to "grow back" quickly without careful supervision.

Teacher Strategy #9:
The Teacher Will Ask Students to Reflect on Their Thinking

Definition: Teacher will ask students to explain the process by which they obtained an answer.

Scenario #9

NONTHOUGHTFUL CLASSROOM	THOUGHTFUL CLASSROOM
Mr. Mix is working on a math problem with his students. The problem involves a rather complicated logic dilemma, where the students have to figure out the final transaction sum. The students discuss the problem at the beginning of class, and a number of possible strategies are suggested by Mr. Mix and the students. The class is working in small cooperative learning groups to figure out the solution. Toward the end of the period, Mr. Mix asks each group to report on their findings. The groups share their answers with the class. Before the bell rings, Mr. Mix tells them the right answer so they can see if they are right.	Mr. Mix is working on a math problem with his students. The problem involves a rather complicated logic dilemma, where the students have to figure out the final transaction sum. The students discuss the problem at the beginning of class, and a number of possible strategies are suggested by Mr. Mix and the students. The class is working in small cooperative learning groups to figure out the solution. Toward the end of the period, Mr. Mix asks each group to report on their findings as well as their process for obtaining their answers. He asks questions like: "How did you figure your answer out?" and "What strategy did you use to obtain that answer?" Students are forced to reflect on their thinking and describe their mental process as much as possible. Different ways for solving the same problems are noted by the teacher and students.

The development of reflective behavior—also known as metacognition—is seen as very important in teaching students to think better. Most writers in the area of teaching thinking invariably mention metacognition as a key component of any program.[19] It can be used during or after any type of thinking activity.

The teacher will ask students to reflect on their thinking.

Ways to Develop Teacher Strategy #9

Metacognition can occur during or after a thinking lesson. You can try some of these techniques: [20]

1—Tell students the thinking skills they are going to use during the lesson.

The purpose of metacognition is to increase students' awareness of their thinking. Labeling and explaining the thinking behavior they are expected to perform will help make them more conscious.

2—At the end of an activity, use metacognitive questioning techniques.

A number of questions can be used:

◆ What strategies (or plan) did you use to reach your conclusion?

◆ What patterns did you see?

◆ How did you _____?

◆ What did you try?

◆ How did you decide _____?

◆ Why did you _____?

3—Have students keep a thinking journal or log.

This journal or log will give students a chance to reflect on their thinking. You can read and comment on the journals.

4—Study the brain.

The study of the brain is an exciting area of science. A number of magazines and television shows have been dedicated to explaining new research on the brain. Letting students study the brain can help them understand what (little) is known of thinking and how it works.[21]

5—Model reflection in front of the students.

Show students how you figured out a problem and then ask them to do the same. Matrix logic problems are good ones to model for students.

6—Teach studying and reading strategies.

Study and reading techniques such as SQR3 and eliminating answers on a test are valuable metacognitive techniques.[22]

7—Post a list of problem-solving strategies.

Students can refer to them before doing a problem; they can also identify the strategy they used after completing a problem. Some common problem-solving strategies to post include

+ working backwards,

+ breaking the problem into smaller pieces,

+ recalling similar problems, and

+ looking for patterns.[23]

Problems You Might Encounter

Finding the time for student reflection can be a big problem. Again, no easy solutions exist for this ever-present problem. Having students write their insights will cut down on class time but increase your grading time. Students can communicate their ideas to each other as they begin to critique and judge each other's thinking.

You will also notice, at first, that students have a difficult time describing their thinking. Their vocabulary is often inexact and vague. They struggle; you will struggle with follow-up questions. Even doing a little bit of metacognition will be helpful. Ask just a few questions—don't demand too much of you or your students at first.

How to Integrate and Develop Teacher Strategies

We have presented nine strategies that, if developed, will increase the amount and level of complex thinking in your classroom. Yet the idea of developing all these strategies may seem overwhelming at first glance—if they don't, think again! Do not, we repeat, *do not* attempt to practice all these strategies at once. You will be setting yourself up for failure and disappointment.

These strategies go against years of teacher training and practice. We are asking many of you to make serious changes in your style and approach to teaching. Indirectly, we are asking your administrators and supervisors to do the same. Change cannot occur overnight. We would like to make a few suggestions for how you might begin to successfully change your teaching style.

Start small. Identify one or two strategies that you would like to tackle. Behaviors that you are already doing partially or that seem easy would be the best to select. Practice those for as long as you wish. A minimum of one year is not an unrealistic expectation for developing a strategy. Use our suggestions as guidelines and add your own ideas.

We have put our suggestions into a table. Each teacher strategy is cited. In the left column, actions that the teacher can take preceding the lesson are given. The central column lists actions taken during the lesson itself. The right column refers the teacher to evaluation tools discussed in chapter 8.

When piloting many of these ideas, we discovered that "wait time," "not repeating student responses," and "no opinions" were the easiest to practice and incorporate into teaching.

TEACHER STRATEGIES
1. THE TEACHER WILL FOCUS AND REFOCUS STUDENTS ON TASK

PREPARATION	LESSON ACTIVITIES	EVALUATING/ IMPROVING
• Write down objectives of the lesson. • Write down the discussion questions. • Focusing questions have characteristics recommended by the Great Books Foundation: (1) teacher has genuine doubt about the answer or answers to the question, (2) teacher cares about the question and (3) teacher writes clear and specific questions.	FOCUSING • Display the main question(s) or problem for students to see. • Have students write a response to the focusing question prior to class discussion. • Use a cognitive map. REFOCUSING • Students write a summary of the discussion. • Hold students accountable for participation with tally sheets. • Continually draw wandering responses back to the initial problem: "How does what you say fit with the original problem?" "How does that help us understand the first question?"	OBSERVATION FORM #1–*Scripting* OBSERVATION FORM #2–*Questioning Behaviors* • Tape record lesson • Videotape lesson • Peer scripting and conferencing

2. THE TEACHER WILL ASK OPEN-ENDED QUESTIONS

PREPARATION	LESSON ACTIVITIES	EVALUATING/ IMPROVING
• List at least three open-ended questions for your lesson. • Use a cognitive map to outline possible progression of the lesson.	• Conduct a specific lesson explaining the use and purpose of open-ended questions. • Teach difference between closed and open-ended questions. • Write questions for students to see during the lesson. CLOSED QUESTIONS When was Ben Franklin born? Is it right for people to steal? What is 5x6? Was life bad during the Civil War? Is a monkey a mammal or reptile? OPEN-ENDED QUESTIONS What was occurring in history at the beginning of Ben Franklin's life? What kinds of stealing are there? Categorize them. Why do you think people passed a law against stealing? What laws would you make for a country about stealing? Tell all the ways you can get the answer 30 using multiplication. Compare life before and after the Civil War. What do monkeys have in common with whales?	OBSERVATION FORM #1–*Scripting* OBSERVATION FORM #2–*Questioning Behaviors* • Use tape recorder to assess teacher questions. • Observe other teachers for questioning. • Practice rewording closed questions to open-ended questions. • Allow assigned students to interrupt the lesson when you ask a "yes-no" question. • Use your peer coach for questioning.

3. THE TEACHER WILL ASK EXTENSION QUESTIONS

PREPARATION	LESSON ACTIVITIES	EVALUATING/ IMPROVING
• Write down a variety of support, extension, or clarification questions to use with students. • Use a cognitive map to outline possible progression of lesson.	• Announce that you will be working on your use of extension questions and will expect the students to stretch their thinking. • Listen to every student response. • Be vigilant about listening for answers that appear vague or unclear. • Use prompting questions: "What do you mean by . . .?" "Please say that in other words." "I'm unclear about . . . ." "Tell us more." "How did you decide?" "Why does that make sense?" "What evidence do you have?" "How does that go with the opening question?" • Do not accept "I don't know." Respond: "I don't know only means you need more time to think. Listen to others and I'll come back to you" (and make sure you do). "Ask me a question that would help you understand." "If you did know what might you say?" "Pretend you do know and make up something."	OBSERVATION FORM#1–*Scripting* OBSERVATION FORM #2– *Questioning Behaviors*

4. THE TEACHER WILL WAIT FOR STUDENT RESPONSES

PREPARATION	LESSON ACTIVITIES	EVALUATING/ IMPROVING
• Prepare tally sheet for observation with students' names.	• Announce that you will be working on wait time. Tell the students what wait time is and why you will practice developing it. • Count to ten to yourself before calling on any student. • Have students share their reactions to the questions with a partner before participating in a large group. • Have students write down responses to a question before you call on anyone. • While you are waiting, demonstrate something or write your question on the board. • Wait until one-half to three-fourths of the students have their hands raised. • Watch students' faces. • Tell students *not* to raise their hands, wait, then call on anyone.	OBSERVATION FORM #3–*Wait Time*

5. THE TEACHER WILL ACCEPT A VARIETY OF STUDENT RESPONSES

PREPARATION

- Make sure the question/problem has several answers.
- Select an observation form best suited to your needs (Student Tally Sheet, Encourage Student Participation). Prepare an observation tally sheet with student names.

LESSON ACTIVITIES

- Announce that you will be looking for a variety of student responses.
- Reserve judgment on responses.
- Students should have several experiences with brainstorming activities.
- Tell students they must participate at least two times (or you decide amount) during a discussion or activity.
- Before calling on anyone, have students write down responses to the questions.
- Use specific questions to encourage variety:
    "What is a totally different answer?"
    "What is another solution?"
    "What are the alternatives?"
    "What are five different ways to . . . ."
- Use cooperative learning techniques and a variety of groupings in your classroom when doing complex-level thinking activities.

EVALUATING/ IMPROVING

OBSERVATION FORM #1–*Scripting*

OBSERVATION FORMS #4a & #4b– *Accepts a Variety of Student Responses*

- Have observer prevent teacher from calling on any one student more than three (or you decide amount) times.

6. THE TEACHER WILL ENCOURAGE STUDENT INTERACTION

PREPARATION

- Arrange seats in a circle for discussion.
- Prepare cooperative learning group.

LESSON ACTIVITIES

- When one student says something, ask another student (or several) to respond to the presented statement.
- Ask students to respond "I agree/disagree with Jeff because . . ." or "Jeff's idea is good and I think . . . ."
- Reduce teacher talk to a minimum.
- Reinforce students when they respond to each other.
- Do regular exercises with your students that develop listening, trust, and discussion skills.
- Use phrases and questions such as: "Who will agree or disagree with Jeff?" "Someone give us a reason why Jeff's idea works." "Does someone have an idea similar to (different from) Jeff's?" "Does Jeff's statement give anyone else any ideas?"
- Direct students to call on one another.
- Periodically require students to paraphrase each other before contributing.

EVALUATING/ IMPROVING

OBSERVATION FORM #4b– *Accepts a Variety of Student Responses*

- Use this form creatively by tallying only for those students who use a phrase that shows they are acknowledging another person's idea.

7. THE TEACHER WILL NOT GIVE OPINIONS OR VALUE JUDGMENTS

PREPARATION	*LESSON ACTIVITIES*	*EVALUATING/ IMPROVING*
• Make a list of your own favorite "nonjudgmental" responses.	• Announce that you will be working on not giving your opinion. • Respond to all students positively but without judgment. Example statements: "That's another idea." "You have been following the discussion." "Your idea seems similar to Jeff's." "Thank you for your idea." "That is thoughtful." • Model nonverbal acceptance of all answers from students by nodding and/or attentively listening. • Write responses on the board or overhead; keep yourself busy so that you don't have time to say "good." • Explain to your students why you are going to stop giving opinions. • Acknowledge all students at the end of the class for the quality of their thinking. • If students ask for your opinion, ask them what they think. Share your opinion only at the *end* of the discussion.	OBSERVATION FORM #5—*Will not give opinions or value judgments/will not repeat student responses* • Tape yourself and count the number of times you give your opinion. Videotape yourself. Look for nonverbal responses that may be judgmental. • At the end of the lesson, acknowledge the entire class. • Acknowledge individuals privately.

8. THE TEACHER WILL NOT REPEAT STUDENT RESPONSES

PREPARATION	*LESSON ACTIVITIES*	*EVALUATING/ IMPROVING*
• Make sure all distracting noises are minimized.	• Tell your students that you will no longer repeat student responses. Tell them why. • Tell students they may tell you if you repeat. • Tell students to raise their hands if they cannot hear another student's comment. • Check for students' hands to be raised. If the response needs to be repeated, ask the *student* to do it. • Replace repeating behaviors with other verbal responses, such as "ok," "uh-huh," or "yes." • Remember that clarifying or rewording the student's comment is a form of repeating.	OBSERVATION FORM #5—*Will not give opinions or value judgments/will not repeat student responses* • Use a tape recorder during a lesson to record yourself. • Use a peer coach (a colleague or friend) who will write down your responses after a student speaks. • Make a videotape focused exclusively on you. Count the number of times you repeat (or reword) for a student.

9. THE TEACHER WILL ASK STUDENTS TO REFLECT ON THEIR THINKING

PREPARATION	LESSON ACTIVITIES	EVALUATING/ IMPROVING
• Post a list of metacognitive skills. • Post a list of problem-solving strategies. • Use a cognitive map to outline your own thinking.	• Tell the students the thinking skills they are going to use during the lesson. • At the end of the lesson, use metacognitive questioning techniques: "What strategies did you use to reach your conclusion?" "What patterns did you see?" "How did you . . .?" "What did you try?" "How did you decide . . .?" "Why did you . . .?" • Have students keep a thinking journal or log. • Study the brain and how it works. • Model reflection in front of the students. • Teach studying and rereading strategies. • Teach students to map their thinking. • Teach students to recognize their individual cognitive strengths.	STUDENT RESPONSE FORM– *Self-evaluation Lesson*

Once you have mastered these strategies, introduce another one. Think of these efforts as long term and continuous. Acknowledge your successes and forgive your mistakes. Be gentle with yourself as you try new things. Remember how long it took you to learn what you are now trying to unlearn! We cannot say enough that developing these strategies will take time and commitment.

Conclusion

We have discussed nine teacher strategies in this chapter that, when used, will lead to more complex thinking in your students. These actions are at the heart of any thinking-skills lesson. You will be surprised and excited by the changes in your students as you begin to practice these strategies in your classroom. Students will become more motivated and empowered. You will become less of an authority of knowledge and more of a facilitator of thinking. In short, your classroom will become more student directed and less teacher directed.

7

The Companions on the Journey: Nine Student Behaviors in the Thoughtful Classroom

Many people would sooner die than think. In fact they do.

Bertrand Russell

The success of our journey toward creating the thoughtful classroom is primarily dependent on the tour guide—the teacher. In the previous chapter, we outlined nine teacher strategies that will encourage complex thinking in the classroom. These teacher strategies, if done consistently and appropriately, will lead to changes in teacher *and* student behavior. For many in the thinking field, it has been enough to discuss the teacher's role. The role of the passengers has been largely neglected or ignored.

Yet, the journey cannot be successful without the active participation of our passengers. In the nonthoughtful classroom, such is not the case; in fact, the teacher may prefer that the students simply get on the tour bus and leave the driving (and everything else) to him or her. In the thoughtful classroom, our ultimate goal is to teach students to take independent trips. The passengers can learn to do this if the roles of both the tour guide and the passengers are clearly defined.

So, what role does the student play in the thoughtful classroom? This question is not a simple one. The student takes his or her cues from the teacher; however, our ultimate goal is to create self-directed, thoughtful students who will spontaneously demonstrate intelligent behaviors in other situations outside the classroom. To reach this goal, students must accept responsibility for their thinking and eventually initiate behaviors that support complex-level thinking.

This chapter will consider the student's role in the thoughtful classroom. Chapter sections will discuss

- ✦ behaviors that students commonly exhibit in the classroom,
- ✦ important student behaviors that promote complex-level thinking,
- ✦ tools to encourage such behaviors, and
- ✦ the relationship between teacher and students in the thoughtful classroom.

Student Behaviors in the Nonthoughtful Classroom

Before looking at students in the thoughtful classroom, let's have a look at what students commonly do. The most customary classroom vehicle for an exchange of thinking is the group discussion. Kids love to talk and many do well with the necessary give and take of a group setting. But students also exhibit an array of behaviors that inhibit the group discussion format. You will recognize some of these:

WALLY (or Wanda) OUTWAITCHA: This student never, but never, raises his hand. When called upon, he can out-wait the most patient teacher and class. He looks down at his desk when called upon. He rolls his eyes up to the ceiling, but in any case he won't answer. He is characterized by his silence in class. He makes no trouble, contributes nothing, and doesn't want to be troubled in return.

CANDY (or Kurt) CUTESEY: Candy always has a cute response, sometimes a joke, sometimes a funny face—almost never on the topic. Candy talks to draw attention to herself. It doesn't matter what she says. It just matters that she is noticed. Her object is to change the objective of this particular lesson.

JOE (or Janey) JUMPATCHA: He's got an answer every time. He's got his hand up every time—higher than anyone else. Often his hand waving is accompanied by rhythmic "I . . . I . . . I . . . know, I . . . know . . . uh . . . uh . . . uh." And he's insatiable. He's the one the teacher relies upon when there are ten minutes left in the period and the discussion is dying.

WENDY (or Wendel) WADJASAY: The teacher can be very sure Wendy is attending but still gets the same response—"Wad ja say?" The teacher repeats the question, only to have Wendy reward the effort with "I da noh."

IAN (or Irene) IDANOH: It has worked for years—"I da noh." How can a teacher respond? If the teacher repeats or clarifies, Ian says, "I don't get it." It is a circle to keep the teacher busy out front so no dangerous thinking can sneak inside.

PAM (or Pete) POMPOUS: This student knows a great deal of content and can talk on most any subject. She'll catch the teacher after class to add to or correct a discussion. She deigns not to talk often in class.

SHANE (or Sharon) SHOENTELL: Teachers avoid this student's hand like the plague. He can kill a discussion just by beginning to speak. Everyone knows that "here comes another account of Shane's personal experiences."

HARRIET (or Harry) HOWSYRWIFE: This student is most often found in upper middle schools or high schools. She will steer the teacher to any topic, keep the teacher talking, and ask leading questions for the sole purpose of pushing the clock beyond the quiz time. She has figured out the lesson plan and knows that if she times it right, she can get to the end of the period without being assigned any work.

There is nothing inherently wrong in any of these responses except that they are impediments to thinking activities. Although these behaviors are most obvious during the group discussion, they are displayed in all learning situations in the classroom. They are mechanisms by which students collectively or individually, intentionally or not, agree not to think—or prevent others from doing so. Some, like Ian Idanoh, Wendy Wadjasay, and Wally Outwaitcha, are obviously avoiding the task. That habit of mental time-out when the discussion gets complex is comfortable but self-defeating.

Some students simply have different agendas for discussion. Students like Shane Shoentell and Candy Cutesey probably have carried on their own class discussions for years. They have become oblivious to the concept that there is a teacher objective. Harriet Howsyrwife is a different story. If you have taught awhile and she can still steer you off task, perhaps this book is not for you.

Pam Pompous and Joe Jumpatcha's participation tends to intimidate the group. Other students justify their own nonparticipation by their perception that Pam and Joe know it all anyhow. These students exude academic self-confidence and may, by verbal or facial expression, belittle the contributions of others.

These student stereotypes have been honed by our teaching system and come in all degrees. Because we all recognize the behaviors so readily, we can be sure that somehow we encourage and reinforce them. We ourselves, if we are honest, remember playing some of these roles. Fortunately, the roles of students in the thoughtful classroom are radically different.

Student Behaviors in the Thoughtful Classroom

Students develop habits of participation. If we don't want our students to continue the old, familiar patterns in the classroom, we must initiate change. There are nine behaviors students need to develop in the thoughtful classroom. The student will

1. participate;
2. give reasons for answers;
3. use precise, specific words;
4. take time to think about the problem and be comfortable with the amount of time a discussion takes;
5. stick with a problem, even though it is difficult;
6. offer different answers to one problem;
7. listen to what other students say;
8. think about his or her thinking; and
9. ask complex-thinking questions about the topic.

Most of these behaviors, which are important in all thinking endeavors, are particularly relevant for classroom discussions. These nine behaviors, if developed and demonstrated by students during thinking activities, will promote complex-level thinking. The familiar behavior patterns presented earlier will begin to be replaced by other, more constructive ways of acting.

Developing the Student Behaviors

The first step in developing these student behaviors is to let students know that they are vital, active partners in the creation of the thoughtful classroom. Your initial role, then, is to enlist them in its development. Such a task may be easier than it first appears.

Students are far more aware than we often suspect; they will already know the game has changed because your behavior is different. So, take time to teach them about the overall concept of the thoughtful classroom— why it is important and what benefits they obtain by agreeing to participate in its establishment. If you believe in the thoughtful classroom—and you must, because you made it to chapter 7!—convincing your students will be easy.

The next step is to *explicitly* teach the students about the nine student behaviors. Do not assume that they will understand what is expected of them by watching you. Informing them about the teacher strategies you are practicing is not enough either. You must inform students about the behaviors they are being asked to demonstrate; in addition, you must tell them that they will be held accountable for successfully mastering these behaviors.

Focusing on both teacher strategies and student behaviors is a demanding task. Do not try to take on more than you can handle. No class should try to focus on all behaviors at one time. Post a sign with these behaviors prominently in the classroom, but select only one or two to actually work on at a time.

After you (and your students, if you desire) have selected the behaviors to develop during the school year, then each chosen behavior should be introduced to the students in a systematic way. One possible method for introducing a student behavior includes the following steps:

1—Define the student behavior.

Read the behavior to the students. Tell them what the behavior means, or work with them to define the behavior in "student words." The behaviors are written with students' understanding in mind; depending on the age group of your class, you may need to simplify or embellish the sentences.

2—Have a class discussion about the behavior.

After you have defined the behavior, talk about it in more detail. If you wish, plan a thinking lesson to discuss the behavior. This suggestion is similar to the one contained in the previous chapter to inform students about the teaching behaviors.

3—Role model the behaviors for the students.

You can demonstrate, with another teacher or with students, how appropriate and inappropriate thinking behaviors might look. For example, you could ask a colleague to help you demonstrate appropriate and inappropriate listening behaviors. Tell the students which behavior you are doing. When modeling appropriate listening, you would nod your head, repeat what you heard, and add to what the other person is saying. You might look away, sigh, or interrupt while displaying inappropriate actions. After you have modeled the behaviors, have the students model for each other.

4—Film the students during a discussion.

The advent of video camcorders makes instant evaluation easy. Taping a discussion or activity and then asking students to evaluate themselves can be a very effective tool.

5—During or after thinking lessons, have the students
    evaluate themselves.

Self-evaluation is a powerful tool, particularly if used on an ongoing basis. Students can keep an evaluation portfolio during the year. Chapter 8 will discuss some possible methods.

These five steps provide a general guideline for initially introducing the behavior. However, there are activities that will help develop each behavior specifically. Some of the ideas we present here are also mentioned in chapter 6; however, we hope to give you more detail on the perspective of developing the *student's*, not the teacher's, behavior. So, let's have a look at each behavior individually.

Student Behavior #1:
The Student Will Participate

An activity or discussion cannot occur unless students participate. The other eight behaviors focus on the *quality* of participation; however, having students take part is the first step to better thinking.

There are three types of participation. Two are overt and measurable, and the third is less overt. First, a student may participate by raising his or her hand to offer input. Second, a student may be called upon by the teacher and answer. Third, a student may do neither but may be actively thinking about the issue.

Tell students about these three methods of participation, and remind them that the overt ways to participate are easiest to credit. You have to get pretty creative and individualize carefully to assess and reward the third type of participation.

This first behavior is the easiest one for students to demonstrate. There are a number of ways to develop it:

1—State the purpose of the lesson clearly.

Students need to know ahead of time what they are expected to do. If the purpose of a discussion is to provide practice and background in a certain thinking skill or content, tell the students your objectives. In addition, the students need to know what they will be expected to do *after* the lesson.

2—Involve the students in keeping track of student responses.

This method was discussed in chapter 6; here is some more detail. Involving students accomplishes a number of objectives. First, students are active participants in the creation of the thoughtful classroom. Second, tallying the number of times each student responds for each discussion gives a picture over time of each student's participation. Students can see their own and the classroom's pattern of participation. The teacher also obtains important information.

The student appointed to tally the day's discussion is excused from the discussion (though we have found he or she often has a hard time "staying out"). Given a class list, the student simply marks each time someone participates. Sometimes, two students can tally at the same time but collect two different types of data. One person tallies participation only if the participant has his or her hand raised when called upon. The second student records when students are called upon without their hand raised. Students can also inform the teacher if any students are called on more than a certain number of times. This monitors the teacher's tendency to focus on eager students who may monopolize the discussion.

3—Put students into different groupings.

Grouping students for complex-level thinking lessons is very important. The size of a group can influence participation. A large group may intimidate some students and make speaking difficult. In addition, the larger the group, the less often each person has the opportunity to speak. Simply cutting the size of the group can increase individual participation.

Different kinds of grouping are available. Students can be grouped in twos or threes. Practice cooperative learning techniques as much as possible.[1] Try some other types of grouping: for example, we occasionally group the less-verbal students together. This action encourages normally quiet students to participate actively in the discussion.

Problems and Issues

Depending upon the age group, students can find that participating in a discussion with peers makes them very vulnerable. Participation must be encouraged in a nonthreatening way. First indicate that you wish for all to participate orally. Then choose topics that are of high interest yet nonthreatening to the dynamics of the group. Recent points of law and current events are great for generating discussions (e.g., curfew, capital punishment for juveniles and/or adults, animal rights, stealing to feed children). Initially, avoid discussions about developing friendships, dating, or cliques.

Certain ethnic groups and family patterns do not value group participation as we know it in a classroom. Because a child refuses to talk in class or contribute to the group overtly does not necessarily mean that he or she is not participating in the thought process. A private arrangement with such students for written participation or a one-on-one discussion should be made.

Finally, be aware of the physical classroom environment. The ability to hear, and thus participate, varies in different parts of the classroom. Sit in a student desk in different locations when the room is full of students. Have someone else conduct the class. Can you hear? Are there other distractions (e.g., bells, lawn mowers, doors with windows that look out at the hallway, noisy cooler or heater vents)? Once you assess bothersome noise, minimize the distractions. Continue to notice any new ones that may appear during the year.

Student Behavior #2:
The Student Will Give Reasons for Answers

Students are now expected to do more than just participate; they are expected to demonstrate reasoning ability when participating. Teachers can do a number of things with students to develop this behavior:

1—Generate a list of key words or phrases with students that would demonstrate reasoning.

For example: "Capital punishment should not be allowed in our state because . . ." or "Last week we said that heat traveled along metal faster than wood, so I think . . ." After students have created this list, have them practice stating their opinion or observation followed by their reason for it.

Ideally, you want to reduce the number of times you ask for reasons and increase the number of times students spontaneously give them. You may have to ask a lot of extension questions when first starting thinking-skills activities, but with practice, students should begin to share their reasons without prompting.

2—Teach students to think before responding.

Students often answer quickly or don't think at all if they notice other students responding. Telling students you want to hear reasons for their answers before asking them something gives them a clue about what you will accept. Do not allow any raised hands for a period of time, telling the class that this is the time to think of reasons for their answers.

Problems and Issues

The biggest problem will occur when students offer reasons without thought. Take the previous example: "Capital punishment should not be allowed in our state because I don't think it is a good idea." This type of response is common. The student says something quickly or uses circular, faulty reasoning. When this happens, continue to probe or, even better, have other students begin to push for more from the student.

Student Behavior #3:
The Student Will Use Precise, Specific Words

This is a difficult behavior for most students. "Stuff" and "thing" and "you know" punctuate student language (and adult language as well). Access to a wide range of vocabulary facilitates precise word usage, so some students have a clear advantage. Yet all students can become more precise when talking. Help students develop this behavior with a number of techniques:

1—Model precise speaking.

This simply means that you are conscious of your own use of language when talking. Precise speaking is easier when you have planned your lesson in advance and know your focusing questions as well as the overall aim of the lesson.

2—Emphasize to students that they must speak concisely.

Say to your students: "Put your thoughts in a nutshell" or "Don't use a lot of words when fewer words will say what you mean."

3—Encourage students to think about what they are going to say before saying it.

Many students and adults think "out loud" in order to help themselves understand. Be patient and respect the time it takes students to get ideas out. Modeling patience tells all students to respect everyone's right to generate a thoughtful statement.

4—Use the vocabulary in the thinking lesson at other times.

Listen for new words. Keep a list in the classroom. Incorporate them into spelling or other language-arts activities.

Problems and Issues

Within the classroom there is a wide range of sophistication in vocabulary. Each student has a certain vocabulary load at his or her fingertips. A student with limited vocabulary will have a difficult time using precise, specific words, while a student with a strong vocabulary may have a difficult time shortening responses. It is a sticky wicket to encourage talking from some students while attempting to pare down the wordiness of others.

Student Behavior #4:
The Student Will Take Time to Think about the Problem and Will Be Comfortable with the Amount of Time an Activity Takes

We want students to learn to ponder a topic before speaking or writing. Like most of the behaviors, this one does not come easily. The teacher must model patience and reward perseverance. Students will quickly cue into the impatience of the teacher.

When students take time to think about a problem, the discussion or activity will take longer than usual. Students can become uneasy or impatient. When they do so, complex thinking will lessen.

Develop this student behavior in the following ways:

1—Remind students before the discussion or activity to think about the problem.

If students are reminded during the discussion, their thinking can be disrupted and slowed. A reminder at the beginning of the lesson is appropriate.

2—Start with short activities and eventually increase the amount of time.

You will be most successful in changing behavior if you start with tiny steps. Reinforce students for a short, successful activity and gradually increase the length of time.

Problems and Issues

The greatest problem was mentioned briefly in the introduction to this behavior—students' impatience. Students will become restless, move in their seats, or talk about being bored. Many of us will hurry up the activity, particularly if we are insecure about the new behaviors we are practicing. Resist caving in to the subtle pressures your students put on you. Remember, change takes time, and you must be willing to have some disgruntled students initially.

Student Behavior #5:
The Student Will Stick with a
Problem, Even Though It Might Be Difficult

Remember, this is the generation brought up on fast food and quick video games. Too much has come too fast and too easily for all our children. Children give up quickly or complain when presented with a complex issue.

We too, as adults, experience this phenomenon. How quickly do you give up on a challenging problem? Perhaps more quickly than you would like to admit! Asking students to take time to think about a problem means that we must be willing to give them time as well. This behavior can be encouraged in a number of ways:

1—Discuss the reasons why people quit when faced with a problem.

After discussing the reasons, have students generate strategies for not quitting. Post these strategies somewhere.

2—Present increasingly difficult problems.

Start with an easy problem. Once the students solve it, reinforce the short amount of time it took. Give increasingly difficult problems, always reinforcing their efforts and success.

Problems and Issues

This behavior is closely related to the one previously discussed, and many of the same issues will occur. Impatience on the part of you or your students will disrupt complex thinking. Sometimes the biggest problem is your own adjustment to the amount of time needed.

Student Behavior #6:
The Student Will Offer Different Answers to One Problem

Offering different answers—divergent thinking—requires the ability to think of more than one solution or insight to a particular problem. Students will sometimes stop after one answer, particularly if the given answer is reinforced by the teacher. Numerous workbooks claim to develop divergent thinking, but they are most often unrelated to the classroom content. The task is to develop this behavior within the context of class assignments. Two key ideas might help achieve this goal:

1—Use the questions suggested in chapter 6 (see pages 72-73, 80).

For example, ask students: "What is another answer to my question?" or "How might you answer this question differently?" or "How many different answers can we think of?"

2—Tell students to write down a certain number of
    answers before speaking.

You can collect these responses at the end of the activity to assess the variety of answers from individual students.

Problems and Issues

One thing students will do when pressed for a variety of answers is offer the same answer with slightly different wording. For example, their first answer might be: "She ran away because her father didn't like her." When asked for a second reason, the student might respond: "Her father hated her, so she left." Writing answers on the board and asking students to notice which ones are the same, only in different words, alerts you and your students to possible repeating.

Student Behavior #7:
The Student Will Listen to What Other Students Say

This behavior is one of the hardest to encourage. Students are trained from kindergarten to listen to the teacher and not to their peers. We discussed a number of ways to develop this behavior under encouraging student interaction in chapter 6, including standing in different parts of the room and not repeating responses. However, there are a number of additional tricks you might try:

1—Engage in listening activities with students.

Before engaging in serious thinking activities with students, locate listening activities for practice. See the references cited in chapter 6 for developing discussion skills.

2—Use questioning strategies.

Sample questions might include: "Please say what Donna said in your own words" or "Who would like to respond to Tom's contention?"

3—Have the students act as teacher.

This suggestion would not work with younger students; however, with high-school students you could expect them to conduct the class. Such an activity can be very empowering for all involved. It will be most successful if you remove yourself from the lesson as much as possible.

4—Teach students to acknowledge each other.

Model and encourage students to say: "According to Mary, . . ." or "I agree with Mary's idea that . . ." or "I disagree with the statement made by Mary earlier because . . ." This is a way for you to turn the thinking back to the students and a way for students to demonstrate that they are listening to one another.

Problems and Issues

Students are highly resistant to listening to anyone but the teacher. They have developed a number of defense mechanisms that make it difficult for them to listen to each other. Instead of asking a student to repeat a response, they will wait expectantly for you to do it. Students will claim that "Maria" is not talking loud enough. They may also be unwilling to disagree with another student.

All of these behaviors will surface when you ask students to listen to each other. Do not become discouraged. Even during your frustration, try to remember that students honestly do not know how to do it differently. Do not enable your students by repeating answers; with time and practice, students will eventually begin to listen to each other.

Student Behavior #8:
The Student Will Think about His or Her Thinking

The ability to think about one's thinking is an advanced mental activity, and it takes practice to develop. However, teaching students to think about their thinking has been strongly advocated by most practitioners and theorists in this field. It can be done in any content area before, after, or during a lesson. A number of student activities can help develop metacognition:

1—Teach students to map their thinking.

A number of people have suggested mapping as a way for students to reflect on the type of thinking they are using.[2] Maps have also been called "graphic outlines" or "organizers."[3] Webbing is a common example of mapping.* With webbing, a central idea is placed in a circle in the middle of the board or a piece of paper. Students generate related ideas or questions extending out from the central idea, much like individual spokes of a wheel. Webbing can be used as a brainstorming technique or as an organizational tool.

2—Teach students to recognize their individual cognitive strengths.

All people have different learning styles. Students can learn their cognitive strengths by assessing learning styles and can then approach thinking accordingly. There are a number of resources available for teaching students about their cognitive styles.[4]

3—Ask questions that probe students' thinking.

After a thinking lesson, make sure to ask students *how* they worked out their solution or strategy. Metacognitive questions can include:

+ How did you _____ ?
+ What did you try?
+ How did you decide _____ ?
+ Why did you _____ ?
+ How do you know that _____ ?
+ How did you happen to _____ ?[5]

4—Have students explain their thinking to each other.

Use a pair-share technique whereby students pair with a partner to describe their thinking to each other.

Problems and Issues

Students are very reluctant to think about their thinking when first pushed. Do not be surprised when you encounter the inevitable shrug coupled with "I don't know." The best way to increase the metacognitive abilities of students is to do so consistently. However, start small. Ask fairly easy questions, and then increase the complexity as students become more fluent with describing their thinking. You can also model metacognition for students. In addition, develop vocabulary for students to use when talking about their cognition.

---

*As we mentioned in chapter 6, mapping techniques can also be used by teachers when planning thinking lessons.

Student Behavior #9:
The Student Will Ask Complex Questions about the Topic

One of the myths of teaching thinking is that if students think more, they are thinking better. But, just having thinking discussions and activities does not necessarily guarantee better thinking. However, one sure way you will know if students are engaging in complex-level thinking is to have them produce complex questions about the topic.

How would you know when your students were asking complex questions? A complex question

+ cannot be answered by yes or no;

+ is original—in other words, the question was not repeated by someone else or taken from the source of the discussion; and

+ requires you and the other students to think before answering.

This behavior is highly sophisticated. For some students, it may take years to develop. In the typical classroom, the teacher asks the questions. Students' questions are limited to procedural or basic-level questions. Try some of these ideas to develop student questioning skills:

1—Play 20 questions.

Although this game can be simplistic, students can begin to learn how to ask questions about a topic.

2—Try "I'll give you the answer and you give me the question."

Such an activity can be done with any type of content or as a quick, fun warmup.

3—Use a thinking matrix to develop students' questions.

This matrix, shown on page 113, is described in an article in *Educational Leadership:* "The vertical axis of the matrix contains symbols of types of thought; the horizontal axis lists categories that give points of departure for inquiry, which vary according to subject area. For example, using the matrix in language arts, teachers or students point to an intersection such as *cause/effect* and *event* or *character* and ask a question about the causes of the hero's death."[6]

THINKTRIX

Thinking Types	DEPARTURE POINTS							
	Char-acter 1	Topic or Event 2	Theme or Con-cept 3	Story 4	Fact 5	Prob-lem 6	Setting 7	Rela-tion-ship 8
R Recall **a**								
Cause-Effect **b**								
Similarity **c**								
Differences **d**								
Idea to Example(s) **e**								
Example(s) to Idea **f**								
Evaluation **g**								

Reprinted with permission from J. McTighe, and F. T. Lyman, Jr. (1988). "Cueing Thinking in the Classroom: The Promise of Theory-embedded Tools."*Educational Leadership* 45, p. 19.

4—Teach students Bloom's taxonomy.

Bloom's taxonomy is an easy way to teach kids about complex-level thinking behaviors. Once you teach students the three higher levels—analysis, synthesis, and evaluation—they can generate questions at each level for a particular topic. Students can also develop their own test questions. A list of verbs for each level can be given to students. We have included a sample list.

BLOOM'S TAXONOMY OF THINKING LEVELS AND CUE WORDS

LEVEL	CUE WORDS			
KNOWLEDGE *Recall* Remembering previously learned material	Observe Repeat Label/Name Cluster	Record Match Memorize	Recall Score List	Recount Sort Outline/Format Stated Define
COMPREHENSION *Translate* Grasping the meaning of material	Paraphrase Tell Report Express	Explain Review Cite Document/ Support	Precise/ Abstract Summarize Restate Describe	Recognize Locate Identify
APPLICATION *Generalize* Using learned material in new and concrete situations	Select Use Manipulate Sequence	Show/ Demonstrate Frame How to Apply	Organize Imitate Dramatize	Illustrate Test Out/Solve Imagine/ Information Known
ANALYSIS *Break Down/Discover* Breaking down material into its component parts so that it may be more easily understood	Examine Classify Distinguish/ Differentiate Outline/No Format Given Conclude/Draw Conclusions	Relate To Characterize Compare/ Contrast (Similarities/ Differences)	Question Research Interpret Analyze	Infer Map Refute Debate/Defend
SYNTHESIS *Compose* Putting material together to form a new whole	Propose Plan Compose	Formulate Design Construct	Emulate Imagine/ Speculate Create	Imagine Invent
EVALUATION *Judge* Judging the value of material for a given purpose	Compare Pro/Cons Prioritize/Rank Judge Decide	Rate Evaluate Criticize Argue	Justify Persuade Assess Value	Convince Predict

5—Ask students: "What don't we know that we should or might want to know?"

Use this question to introduce a topic. For example, if you are starting to study genetics, you might write the word on the board and ask students to generate a list of questions to answer on this topic. These questions can then be used for research topics.

6—Teach students "question starters."

Students can learn the difference between open and closed questions in much the same way you did. First, teach them that starting a question with "Is . . ." or "Do you . . ." will lead to little thinking. Then, teach them to start questions with words such as "Why . . ." or "If . . ." or "How might . . .". Keep a list of good and bad question starters easily available in your room.

As with several of the other behaviors, it may be difficult to develop this behavior in one school year. Students believe that when you ask a question you are "dumb." They need to learn that it is okay to ask questions, that, in fact, you *want* them to! Students will need years of practice. Begin with easy, basic questions and increase the difficulty as students become more proficient. Remember, too, that good questions come from having enough knowledge about a topic to ask them. Point out to the students when they ask good questions; you might keep a list posted with good questions on it. Investigate other sources that focus on how to teach students to become better questioners.[7]

The Relationship between Student Behaviors and Teacher Strategies

Obviously, student behaviors and teacher strategies are connected. For most of the teacher strategies, there is a set of corresponding student behaviors. The following chart illustrates this relationship.

Teacher Strategies and Corresponding Student Behaviors

Teacher Strategies	*Corresponding Student Behaviors*
1. The teacher will focus and refocus students on task.	The student will stick with a problem, even though it might be difficult.
2. The teacher will ask open-ended questions.	The student will offer different answers to one problem.
3. The teacher will ask extension questions.	The student will give reasons for answers.
4. The teacher will wait for student responses.	The student will use precise, specific words.
5. The teacher will accept a variety of student responses.	The student will take time to think about a problem and will be comfortable with the amount of time an activity takes.
6. The teacher will encourage student interaction.	The student will offer different answers to one problem.
7. The teacher will not give opinions or value judgments.	The student will listen to what other students say.
8 The teacher will not repeat student responses.	The student will listen to what other students are saying.
9. The teacher will ask students to reflect on their thinking.	The student will think about his or her thinking.
	The student will ask complex thinking questions about the topic.

There is only one teacher strategy, *the teacher will not give opinions or value judgments,* that does not elicit a corresponding student behavior. While there isn't an immediate parallel student behavior, we believe there is a long-term result. Saying "great" or "that's an excellent point" tends to shut down the thinking of students not receiving the praise. *The student will ask complex thinking questions about the topic* and *the student will participate* are the only student behaviors that do not correspond directly to a teacher strategy. Yet these student behaviors will be influenced positively by all the teacher strategies and student behaviors.

When you select a teacher strategy to work on, select a complementary student behavior for your class. Evaluation will be easier and the relationship between what you are doing and what your students are doing will be clear to all involved.

As teachers change their behavior and strategies, students will, in turn, change. The behaviors exhibited by the Shane Shoentells and the Candy Cuteseys will not totally disappear, but new behaviors will emerge. As you and your students benefit from the thoughtful classroom, old behaviors will be less important in daily class activities. People do not continue behaviors that profit them little.

Even though the teacher must implement change before the students do, we believe that students can begin to take responsibility for their behavior too. With modeling and prompting, students can take responsibility for becoming better thinkers.

To help you achieve this end, we have included charts summarizing the behaviors discussed in this chapter. These charts are for your students. Each behavior is listed with ideas on what the students can do during and after the lesson to improve their thinking ability. Copy these charts and let your students use them.

Conclusion

In this chapter, a number of specific student behaviors and how to develop them were discussed. Although the student takes direction from the teacher, our goal is to create self-directed thinkers. Our intent in dedicating a chapter to student behaviors, even though there is overlap with chapter 6, is to reinforce the notion that the student has responsibility in the thoughtful classroom too.

1. I WILL PARTICIPATE

DURING THE LESSON

- Listen to the focusing question.
- Think about what other students say.
- Try to give an answer when called upon.
- If you cannot comment say, "I need more time to think (listen)."
- Be aware of the number of times you participate.
- If oral participation is difficult, you should ask the teacher if you may participate by writing answers.

EVALUATING & IMPROVING MY THINKING

- STUDENT SELF-EVALUATION–*Lesson*

  Your teacher will sometimes have you fill out a self-evaluation. Be honest.

- STUDENT RESPONSE FORM–*Tally Participation*

  If your teacher has a student tallying responses, ask to see how many times you participated.

- AFTER SCHOOL:

  Discuss news items with your parents. Get their point of view. Don't judge or give opinions—simply listen for another person's point of view. Ask for their reasons.

NOTES TO MYSELF:

_____

_____

_____

_____

2. I WILL GIVE REASONS FOR ANSWERS

DURING THE LESSON

- Ask for clarification of focusing question/problem if you don't understand.
- Ask questions about the focusing question.
- Take a stand on one idea (answer).
- Write down possible reasons for your idea
  or
- Think about reasons before speaking.
- Listen to other people's reasons.
- Give reasons when called upon, using the sentence structure for reason statements.

EVALUATING & IMPROVING MY THINKING

- STUDENT SELF-EVALUATION–*Lesson*
- STUDENT RESPONSE FORM–*Gives Reasons*

AFTER SCHOOL:

- Practice giving reasons for your opinions.
- Identify opinion and fact when you listen to TV programs.
- Practice using the sentence structure for reason statements:
- "I believe _____ because (*reason*)."

NOTES TO MYSELF:

_____

_____

_____

_____

3. I WILL USE PRECISE, SPECIFIC WORDS

DURING THE LESSON

- Teacher will model precise speaking, so listen to the teacher.
- Think about what you wish to say before saying it.
- Try to speak concisely: Put your thoughts in a "nutshell."
- Take opportunities to practice speaking in a small group as well as in total class.
- Try not to use "you know."
- Note new vocabulary you hear.
- Use new vocabulary in other situations.

EVALUATING & IMPROVING MY THINKING

- STUDENT SELF-EVALUATION–*Lesson*
- STUDENT RESPONSE FORM–*Using Precise, Specific Words*
- Ask a partner to script your responses in a discussion. After discussion attempt to reword your response for precision and clarity.
- Practice rewording verbose sentences in writing.
- Practice rewording another person's statements orally.
- Listen for precision in teacher's speech.

NOTES TO MYSELF:

_____

_____

_____

_____

4. I WILL TAKE TIME TO THINK ABOUT THE PROBLEM AND WILL BE COMFORTABLE WITH THE AMOUNT OF TIME AN ACTIVITY TAKES

DURING THE LESSON

- Concentrate on the problem.
- If you can't hear, raise your hand and ask for the student to repeat.
- Think about several solutions/answers to the question.
- If you start to daydream, write down a few thoughts about the issue.
- Actively listen to other students and think about what they are saying.

EVALUATING & IMPROVING MY THINKING

- STUDENT SELF-EVALUATION–*Lesson*

- Be familiar with the requested student behaviors.

AFTER SCHOOL:
- Spend "quiet time" at home with no TV.
- Read, plan something you will do, think about something that happened.

NOTES TO MYSELF:

_____

_____

_____

_____

5. I WILL STICK WITH A PROBLEM, EVEN THOUGH IT IS DIFFICULT

DURING THE LESSON

- Decide not to quit even if you don't understand.
- Listen for the parts you do understand.
- Work increasingly difficult problems.
- Talk to other students about how they solve problems.

EVALUATING & IMPROVING MY THINKING

- STUDENT SELF-EVALUATION–Lesson

AFTER SCHOOL:

- Do puzzles, models, or such projects at home.
- Work alone on something.
- Ask directions and attempt to figure things out for yourself.
- Practice not quitting in sports.
- Try to be independent in work.
- Define the characteristics of successful people.

NOTES TO MYSELF:

_____
_____
_____
_____

6. I WILL OFFER DIFFERENT ANSWERS TO ONE PROBLEM

DURING THE LESSON

- Listen for open-ended questions and ask yourself:

    "How many ways can that be answered?"

    "What is something no one has said yet?"

    "How would my dad (mom, brother) answer that?"

    "What's an angle the teacher has not yet thought of?"

- Write down several answers before volunteering answers.

EVALUATING & IMPROVING MY THINKING

- STUDENT SELF-EVALUATION–Lesson

- STUDENT RESPONSE FORM–Offering Different Answers to One Problem

NOTES TO MYSELF:

_____
_____
_____
_____

7. I WILL LISTEN TO WHAT OTHER STUDENTS SAY

DURING THE LESSON

- Look at the person who is speaking.
- Think about what the other person is saying.
- Agree or disagree in your mind as you listen to others.
- Preface your comments by acknowledging other students' ideas when appropriate:

  "Jeff made me think of something . . ."

  "I disagree with Jeff because . . ."

  "I wonder if Jeff ever thought of this situation . . ."

- Remember that disagreeing with a person's comments does not mean you find the *person* disagreeable.
- Separate your personal feelings from the discussion. Because you do not "hang around" with another student does not mean that you should not listen to that person's ideas.
- Sometimes reword another person's thoughts. For example:

  "I believe I understood Jeff to say . . ."

  "Do I understand you, Jeff, to mean . . ."

- Do not interrupt another person.
- Try not to raise your hand while another person is talking.
- Comment on other people's statements only to the group—no side comments.
- Be supportive of each other in their comments:

  "I see Jeff's point, but I believe . . ."

EVALUATING & IMPROVING MY THINKING

- STUDENT SELF-EVALUATION–*Lesson*

- STUDENT RESPONSE FORM–*Tally for Acknowledging Other Students*

AFTER SCHOOL:

- Practice REALLY listening to your best friend.
- Practice these behaviors at home with parents.
- Listen to an assigned newscast, without taking notes, and write a synopsis.

NOTES TO MYSELF:

_____

_____

_____

_____

_____

_____

_____

_____

8. I WILL THINK ABOUT MY THINKING

DURING THE LESSON

- Be able to tell how you solved a problem (not telling the answer).
- Be aware of how you are thinking.
- Try to understand how another person is figuring out a problem.
- Map your thinking.
- Study the brain.

EVALUATING & IMPROVING MY THINKING

- STUDENT SELF-EVALUATION–*Lesson*
- Find a younger child, present him or her with a problem, and ask the child to tell how he or she solved it. Explain how to solve the problem to the child.
- Tell what you thought about to answer the problem of how to _____.
- List the things you are best at naturally.
- Think about "nothing" and write about what happens in three minutes.
- Discuss dreams, déjà vu, premonitions, and other mental occurrences.
- Discuss mental characteristics of your parents, brothers, sisters, and friends and relate them to yourself.
- Compare your method to a partner's method of solving a problem.

NOTES TO MYSELF:

_____

_____

_____

9. I WILL ASK COMPLEX QUESTIONS ABOUT THE TOPIC

DURING THE LESSON

During the discussion:

1. Listen for parts of the topic you do understand.
2. Compare the topic to other things you know.
3. Listen to what other people are asking.

When asking a complex question:

1. Begin the question with words like **how, why, what, if.** Sample questions could be:

    a. **How is this different from . . . ?**
    b. **How does this compare to . . . ?**
    c. **What caused . . . ?**

EVALUATING & IMPROVING MY THINKING

- STUDENT SELF-EVALUATION–*Lesson*
- STUDENT RESPONSE FORM–*Asking Complex Questions*

AFTER SCHOOL:

- Ask your parents or brothers and sisters questions about something they know that you don't.

NOTES TO MYSELF:

_____

_____

_____

8

Evaluating the Thoughtful Classroom:
Reflecting on the Ultimate Journey

As I grow older, I pay less attention to what men say.
I just watch what they do.

Andrew Carnegie

We have arrived at the last chapter, but we are nowhere near the end of our journey. The commitment to create the thoughtful classroom is lifelong. Once we take the beginning steps as described in the first seven chapters, we will not want to stop our travels. The rewards and benefits you and your students will receive as you engage in regular, disciplined inquiry will far exceed the obstacles you must overcome to infuse thinking into your curriculum.

Every year, you and your students create the thoughtful classroom together. As the tour guide, you take a similar journey every year, but your companions on the trip eventually have to go on without you. Yet the end of the school year is not the end of the journey for either you or your students. Your students have now experienced the challenge and triumph of regular, thoughtful discourse; in other words, they see themselves as "thinkers." With increasing school reform and a little luck, they will continue to find other thoughtful classrooms. Your job is to continue to refine and improve the part of the trip they take with you, so that each year is an even better journey.

You change and refine through evaluation. When assessing the thoughtful classroom, your main job is to decide whether you are (a) teaching the content and thinking skills you wish to teach and (b) performing the teacher strategies. You also need to assess whether your students are demonstrating the corresponding student behaviors. Therefore, this chapter focuses on how teachers can use evaluation effectively.

Some General Observations
concerning the Evaluation of Thinking

Evaluate can be defined as "to ascertain, judge, or fix the value or worth of."[1] When you evaluate yourself, you have the underlying belief that you can be better at what you do. Also, you possess a strong commitment to creating the thoughtful classroom, because without knowing what you do and don't do well, you can never change. However, having a commitment to improve is the easy part. The actual act of evaluating is much harder. Thinking is notoriously difficult to evaluate; consequently, the topic of evaluating complex-level thinking is frequently overlooked or ignored. A number of reasons can be given for this lack of attention.

First, engaging in evaluation is a fearful thing for many of us. By its very definition, evaluation implies judgment about what we did or didn't do. In the teaching profession, evaluation, overt or covert, has been used to pass judgment and to label—not for constructive change. Evaluation is the last thing on everyone's mind. It's the end of a lesson, the end of the year, the last day of the week, and the last to be funded. Because evaluation is the hardest to do, it is considered only after all the energy and funds are spent on the "first" part.

The main reason, however, for the lack of evaluation tools is that no one knows how to effectively evaluate whether students are thinking on complex levels. This problem is akin to the ancient fable of the blind men and the elephant. The blind men evaluated different parts of the mammoth; yet their individual descriptions could not produce a concept of the whole creature. The men of the fable couldn't see, but they could at least touch. As we noted in chapter 3, we can neither see nor touch thinking (i.e., "our elephant").

However, despite the problems associated with evaluation, such an undertaking is critical to the success of the thoughtful classroom. Evaluators often talk about formative and summative evaluation, the former being collected on an ongoing basis and the latter being gathered to assess final outcomes. Discussions center on when to use summative and formative evaluation.

Both are necessary. Evaluation should take place throughout the year so that the teacher can make changes as needed. However, at the end of the year, the formative data can be analyzed and used to report on overall changes. In addition, summative data (e.g., pre- and posttests) can be compiled for outcome data.

When to collect data is only one issue. Each of us interested in implementing a thoughtful curriculum must decide *what* is important to evaluate. One must decide whether to focus on the cognitive tasks students engage in (i.e., content and thinking processes) or on the behaviors that the teacher and students show that are indicative of intelligent, thoughtful people.

Although we discuss content and thinking processes and teacher strategies and student behaviors separately, they are, of course, interrelated. We know, from some research, that teacher strategies can encourage complex-level thinking in students. Therefore, if you assess content and thinking processes in students, you may also be gathering information about teacher strategies. For example, if the students score high on posttests of complex-level thinking, the assumption can be made that the teacher is doing something to aid such performances. Conversely, if you are evaluating teacher strategies and student behavior, then you may also be indirectly gathering information about whether students are learning to think better. (If teachers consistently practice wait time, for example, then the complexity of student responses should increase over time.)

Therefore, information about both areas can be used for improvement and change. In the next section, we will consider the two primary avenues available to teachers for evaluating complex-level thinking: norm-referenced methods and criterion-referenced methods. Within each category, we will discuss the evaluation of both content and thinking processes and the behaviors teachers and students demonstrate during thinking lessons.

Norm-Referenced Evaluation Instruments

Norm-referenced techniques for evaluating thinking have appeared in the past several years. These evaluation methods are "normed" on a population representative of the group that is taking the test. Therefore, a norm-referenced instrument provides a standard to judge the performance of a classroom against the performance of a larger group that represents the norm of the nation. These materials are commercially published and are available for immediate use.

Norm-Referenced Instruments for Assessing Content and Thinking Processes

Most of the available instruments assess the outcomes of a thinking curriculum and are used for pre- and posttest measurement. These tests are group measures, giving you information about students' ability to perform certain thinking tasks, and they would be considered process tests. They do not provide information about the conceptual understanding of content, the *teaching* of thinking, or teacher and student behavior during thinking lessons. A sampling of the available thinking-process tests follows:[2]

1. *The Watson-Glaser Critical Thinking Appraisal.*[3] This test is used with grade 9 and above and contains five subtests.

2. *The Cornell Critical Thinking Test.*[4] This test is based on Ennis's theories of critical thinking and is appropriate for grades 7–12. Level Z can be used with college students.

3. *The New Jersey Test of Reasoning Skills, Form B.*[5] This test was designed to assess skills and processes taught in the *Philosophy for Children* thinking program, and can be used with grades 4 through college.

4. *The SEA Test.*[6] This test was designed to evaluate students' ability to perform the higher levels of Bloom's taxonomy, including analysis, synthesis, and evaluation.

The benefits of using norm-referenced tests for evaluating thinking are those inherent in any standardized test. They can be obtained easily and require little extra teacher time. The only time needed is for administration and scoring. The results will be normed, thereby providing information about how students perform compared to their peers.

Several disadvantages can be noted. Norm-referenced materials cost money—a commodity many of us do not have. Perhaps the biggest difficulty is the limited range of the test. First, little diagnostic information can be gained. Second, for the information to be useful, you must be teaching the skills or processes the test purports to measure. So, for example, if you use *The SEA Test*, it would be necessary to be teaching the skills of evaluation, analysis, and synthesis. In other words, there must be a match between your curriculum objectives and the test's focus. Such a requirement can limit your curriculum.

Selma Wassermann, who has been interested in the thinking field for some time, reflects on the use of thinking measures in a wonderful article.[7] She notes a number of difficulties associated with using standardized measures of thinking, including the personal value systems we bring to our decisions about what test to use, the rigidity of tests, and the difficulty of assessing the complex act of thinking.*

Two concerns need to be mentioned.[8] Research indicates that many of the available tests do not easily distinguish between the different hypothesized mental skills (e.g., tests might not show the difference between predicting consequences and making hypotheses). Also, many of the available tests correlate very highly with intelligence measures, suggesting that the two types of tests are, in fact, testing the same thing. Such a conclusion renders thinking tests useless as a separate assessment tool.

---

*She, like us, advocates the use of observation tools. We will be covering those in the next section.

Few, if any, norm-referenced instruments directly assess the types of teacher strategies and student behaviors discussed extensively in chapters 6 and 7. Although both research and common sense support the need for changes in teacher strategies, the data that would be needed to create a norm for tests on such behaviors has not been collected.

However, one test, *The Class Activities Questionnaire* (CAQ), could be utilized as a possible measure.[9] The CAQ was originally developed to assess classroom climate and the teaching of higher-level thinking in Illinois gifted programs. The CAQ assesses five major dimensions of classroom climate: lower thought processes, higher thought processes, classroom focus, classroom climate, and student opinions. Although designed for use with gifted students, the CAQ could be used in regular classrooms, 6–12, to assess both the thinking skills being taught and the classroom climate. Then, information about the classroom climate can provide useful insights into teacher strategies.

Each dimension has a number of factors. For example, the higher thought processes dimension contains application, analysis, synthesis, and evaluation. The two thinking dimensions are, in fact, based on Bloom's taxonomy. The classroom climate dimension assesses the factors of enthusiasm, independence, divergence, humor, ideas valued, ideas enjoyed, teacher talk, and homework. The first page of the CAQ is shown on page 127.

Both the teacher and the students can take the CAQ. Then the teacher can compare his or her perceptions with those of the students. The information can be used in either a summative or a formative manner. Students can also be informed of the results. Changes can be made as necessary.

Because there are so few norm-referenced instruments for assessing the thoughtful classroom, it is obvious that other avenues must be explored if evaluation is to be successful. Many of us must use criterion-referenced materials to meet our needs.

CLASS ACTIVITIES QUESTIONNAIRE

For each sentence below, circle the letters which show the extent to which you AGREE or DISAGREE.

Circle **SA** if you **STRONGLY AGREE** with the sentence.

Circle **A** if you **AGREE** moderately with the sentence.

Circle **D** if you **DISAGREE** moderately with the sentence.

Circle **SD** if you **STRONGLY DISAGREE** with the sentence.

Base your answer on how well each sentence describes what is stressed in your class—what your teachers ask you to do.

1. Remembering or recognizing information is the student's main job.	SA	A	D	SD
2. A central activity is to make judgments of good/bad, right/wrong, and explain why.	SA	A	D	SD
3. Students actively put methods and ideas to use in new situations.	SA	A	D	SD
4. Most class time is spent doing other things than listening.	SA	A	D	SD
5. The class actively participates in discussion.	SA	A	D	SD
6. Students are expected to go beyond the information given to see what is implied.	SA	A	D	SD
7. Great importance is placed on logical reasoning and analysis.	SA	A	D	SD
8. The student's job is to know the one best answer to each problem.	SA	A	D	SD
9. Restating ideas in your own words is a central concern.	SA	A	D	SD
10. Great emphasis is placed on memorizing.	SA	A	D	SD
11. Students are urged to build onto what they have learned to produce something brand-new.	SA	A	D	SD
12. Using logic and reasoning processes to think through complicated problems (and prove the answer) is a major activity.	SA	A	D	SD
13. A central concern is practicing methods in lifelike situations to develop skill in solving problems.	SA	A	D	SD
14. Students are encouraged to independently explore and begin new activities.	SA	A	D	SD
15. There is little opportunity for students' participation in discussions.	SA	A	D	SD

This is an early version of the *Class Activities Questionnaire.* The newest version is prepared on optical scanning sheets and is reprinted with permission from the publisher. *Class Activities Questionnaire,* Mansfield Center, Conn.: Creative Learning Press, 1981.

Criterion-Referenced Evaluation Instruments

Criterion-referenced measures are those created by teachers or others to assess a particular situation. Teachers can use criterion-referenced tests to evaluate whether students have learned a particular content or process being taught in the class. No norms are available, so it is impossible to compare a specific individual or group performance to a national norm. However, individuals or groups can assess their performance over a period of time, or information can be collected for diagnostic purposes.

Criterion-Referenced Instruments for Assessing Content and Thinking Processes

Teachers can use published criterion-referenced instruments or design their own. Unit tests at the end of textbooks would qualify as criterion-referenced instruments; however, as we noted in chapter 5, most textbooks fail to develop complex-level thinking. Therefore, most criterion-referenced tests for assessing complex-level thinking will be designed by the teacher.

The criterion-referenced evaluation of content and thinking processes that you devise will be influenced by your method of teaching. If you are using the conceptual infusion approach in your classroom, then assessment of thinking will occur as part of the assessment of content. For example, if students are required to compare and contrast Hitler's and Mussolini's personalities after a unit on World War II, then they are, in fact, being asked to demonstrate both content knowledge and thinking skills. When you grade the exams, you will be assessing the students' grasp of the concepts and their ability to think conceptually.

However, be cautious about asking students to use thinking skills you have not taught during the unit or lesson. Using the previous example, asking students to compare and contrast would be appropriate only if you have taught your students to compare and contrast or were confident that they had obtained the skill previously. Here is a simple rule to prevent the danger of assessing your students on material not covered in class: use your lesson plans and units as the guidelines for any exams or tests you design. A good resource for more ideas on developing thinking tests for your classroom is a book published by the National Education Association.[10]

If you are using the direct, or general, method of teaching thinking (see chapter 2, pages 15-16), then the focus of the evaluation will be different. With the direct method, thinking processes are of primary interest; the understanding of content is frequently irrelevant. Published programs based on the direct method often contain assessment tools. However, if you are teaching thinking directly with teacher-designed materials, the responsibility for evaluation falls on you.

Burns gives some useful suggestions on evaluating thinking-skill proficiency with teacher-developed tests.[11] On the test, there should be several test questions that concern the thinking skills that were taught. The test questions should give students the following opportunities to:

1. Define the skill in their own words.
2. Pick, from several options, an example of the skill in use.
3. Critique an imperfect example of the skill's use.
4. Execute the skill while showing or explaining their work.
5. Explain to someone how to use the skill.
6. Use new data, not previously presented in class, to apply the skill.

The benefits of using criterion-referenced tools for assessing process and content are obvious. First, the only cost is time. The tests can be designed to match your particular situation and needs. The main disadvantage can be extrapolated from the advantages mentioned for the norm-referenced tests: criterion-referenced materials give you little information about how your class is doing in comparison to other students.

Criterion-Referenced Tests for Assessing Teacher Strategies and Student Behaviors

Assessing content knowledge and thinking processes is relatively easy compared to assessing teacher strategies and student behaviors. Yet we and others have made a strong case that certain teacher strategies and student behaviors will encourage better complex-level thinking in students. Therefore, it is crucial that we evaluate the strategies and behaviors we discussed in chapters 6 and 7. The next section presents some ideas on how this might be done.

Teacher Strategies

Regardless of the particular strategy being evaluated, the teacher has two choices: to evaluate him- or herself or to work with another person. Self-evaluation is probably the more difficult of the two options because strong discipline and commitment are required. However, self-evaluation can be safer for some teachers when they first begin because of reduced anxiety and fear.

If you want to evaluate yourself, you can begin by keeping a log or journal during the journey. Write down when you teach thinking lessons and your reactions, as well as your students', to the lesson. Notice what worked and what didn't. Keep track of the highlights and the low places of the journey.

The next step in the self-evaluation process is to gain access to either a tape recorder or a video camera. Then tape or record the lesson you wish to evaluate. After you have taped the lesson, rate or judge your performance. If you have followed the suggestions in this book, you will have identified one strategy to develop. Therefore, you will evaluate only one or two strategies when you watch or listen to the tape. After your self-evaluation, the next step is to make adjustments and repeat the self-evaluation. The next section provides you with forms you can use when evaluating yourself.

Working with another person can be difficult at first. Many of us enter the teaching profession so we can work behind "closed doors." A degree of anxiety and insecurity can be expected if you ask someone else to help you on your journey toward the thoughtful classroom. However, the benefits are enormous. First and foremost, you are doing what you are asking your students to do constantly in the thoughtful classroom: take a risk. In addition, you will receive valuable support and encouragement and reduce the constant isolation we can experience as teachers.

Your students or principal can act as evaluators, providing feedback and suggestions for change. However, peer coaching is perhaps the best technique for developing teacher strategies and student behaviors. Peer coaching is an exciting new staff development method being utilized in a variety of educational settings to achieve any number of educational goals. Peer coaching is attractive because the technique removes the stigma and fear surrounding evaluation. When you are being coached by a peer, you are in control of the process from beginning to end. In other words, you, and no one else, determine the value and worth of what you do, thereby eliminating the judgment so often associated with evaluation.

Peer coaching is a simple process. A teacher who wishes to improve a behavior or strategy in the classroom requests someone to act as a "coach." Most often, this coach will be a fellow teacher, although a principal or parent could play this role. Once a coach has been selected, both the coach and the teacher meet to discuss the role of the peer coach and the changes the teacher wishes to work toward. The best way to collect information is decided. The peer coach then sits in the classroom during a lesson for a predesignated period of time, collecting data. A conference is held after the lesson, and the peer coach presents the information that he or she gathered. The peer-coaching process is then repeated for however long is desired.

Peer coaching is a very effective technique for developing the teacher strategies. In fact, Robert Garmston discusses a similar project at the university level that showed great success.[12] For example, let's say you want to work on wait time. You ask a trusted colleague to act as your peer coach. You describe the strategy you wish to work on and provide him or her with the form we describe in the next section. The peer coach comes to your classroom during the thinking lesson and records data. Data can be recorded in a number of ways, including scripting the lesson word for word or tallying certain behaviors. After school, you meet and the peer coach shares the data on wait time.

The peer coach, however, does not assess your wait time ability. For example, the peer coach does not say: "Your wait time today was horrible." *Nor* does the peer coach say: "Your wait time was great today." The job of assessment is yours alone.[13] The peer coach is a recorder of information. Although this type of interaction may seem strange at first, it is crucial to the success of peer coaching. You learn to critically examine your teaching, both the strengths and the weaknesses. Assessing your own behavior is empowering. You, and no one else, become responsible for your behavior.

Peer coaching will work best if you follow a number of guidelines. First, have both an initial meeting and a follow-up conference. Second, do not try to evaluate yourself during an entire lesson; instead, select fifteen minutes that will be a good representation of your teaching behavior. Choose a person you trust and like. Finally, use a peer coach over a consistent period of time. Following is a summary of useful tips for observers and peer coaches.

THE ROLE OF THE OBSERVER: Some Helpful Hints

Keep on the Requested Task:

When you are invited to observe, the teacher depends upon you to focus on the behavior he or she has designated. You must put aside your own interests and focus on those behaviors *only* in order to give as much feedback as possible. Don't get involved in the lesson. Don't begin planning how you could adapt it to your classroom. Focus!

Be Inconspicuous:

The classroom must remain as natural as possible. Make it clear to any student who solicits your attention that you wish to be inconspicuous and attentive to the teacher. The kids will soon get the idea and will learn to ignore you during the lesson. During a thinking lesson, teachers usually let the class know exactly what is going on. The students know what behaviors the teacher is working on and which ones they are trying to improve. A student may even be tallying student responses during the same lesson you are scripting. Generally the teacher will let the students know that you are not scripting them, to alleviate any student concern. Follow the lead of the teacher.

Offer Advice Only If Asked:

Advice, no matter how well intended, is never welcome unless solicited. An invitation to observe may or *may not* be an invitation to critique. IF the teacher asks, you may proceed with your opinion. You need to preface your remarks with the fact that you are expressing your opinion and it should be taken in that context. For true collegiality, observer and teacher should be similar in expertise. If one member has more experience, then the relationship is one of a mentor. Both relationships promote growth—just define the relationship before you begin. The kiss of death on any relationship of this nature is professional rudeness—that is, gossip.

Help the Teacher Stay Focused:

Ideally, you meet soon after the lesson and discuss the scripting. As the observer you may state observations that are pertinent to the observation sheet. After the first observation of a behavior, you may begin to look for patterns and discuss future observations.

Regardless of whether you use a peer or yourself to evaluate, make a videotape of yourself teaching a thinking lesson at the beginning of the year, if at all possible. Then, at the end of the year, make another tape. It can be exciting to see the difference!

Having discussed some general ways of evaluating teacher performance, let's take a closer look at the strategies described in chapter 6 and discuss specific evaluation techniques for each. We have developed a number of forms that can be used for this purpose (see appendix C). The forms summarize each strategy and the techniques that can be used to assess it.*

The teacher will focus and refocus students on task.

This strategy can be assessed by using Observation Form #1 or Observation Form #2. Observation Form #1 is a general scripting form and will be used for other strategies. This form has three columns: time, teacher talk, and student talk. Both teacher and student talk should be recorded when using this form. After the lesson, the content can be assessed for how the teacher focused and refocused the lesson.

Observation Form #2 is more specific. With this form, the observer writes down only the teacher's questions or requests (questions in the form of a command). Questions are then coded as to whether they are open, closed, or irrelevant. The open questions can then be categorized. Teachers can discern whether their students become sidetracked, as well as how many focusing questions they ask.

The teacher will ask open-ended questions.

Observation Form #2 can be used to evaluate this teacher strategy. The technique is identical to the one described above, except the questions and requests are classified as either open or closed. Closed questions are further classified as requiring either a yes/no answer or a fact answer.

The teacher will ask extension questions.

Observation Form #2 can be used for this strategy, too. Teacher questions and requests are written down and then coded. However, for this strategy, coding is more specific. Open questions are coded as to whether they were asking for reasons, seeking different ideas or elaboration, or asking for clarification. William Wilen suggests a similar method of evaluation in his book.[14]

---

*Of course, you do not need a form to script teacher behavior. Any sheet of paper and a writing implement will do. However, we have found that a form lends legitimacy and weight to the task and provides uniformity for your evaluation results.

The teacher will wait for student responses.

Wait time can be assessed using Observation Form #3. The questions and requests given by the teacher are written down. Then, using a watch with a second hand, the observer records the time between when the question is asked and when the teacher calls on someone or the student responds. It can be difficult to record both the time and the question; however, with practice, it becomes easier.

The teacher will accept a variety of student responses.

Two forms can be used for evaluating this strategy, Observation Forms #4a and #4b. Observation Form #4a asks the observer to script the teacher's questions and requests, and then count the number of student responses to that question. Observation Form #4b is a tally sheet. A tally is kept of the number of times each student responds during the discussion.

The teacher will encourage student interaction.

Student interaction can be evaluated by using a map or diagram of the discussion. Both the Great Books Foundation and the Taba Teaching Strategies manuals use diagrams to map student interaction.[15] The Great Books Foundation suggests that you seat your students in a circle and then draw a diagram of where everyone is sitting. As students talk to each other, you can note the interaction patterns by drawing lines between students who talk or by making notes. You can also use this system for other strategies; for example, types of questions can be coded. At the end of the discussion, you will have a clear representation of student interaction.

The Taba manuals recommend using a simple interaction chart. The coding system has two lines of boxes, repeated. The top line is for the teacher strategy, and the bottom is for student behavior. You record the behaviors sequentially as they happen.

For example, the teacher begins the complex-level lesson by asking a question. The observer marks a "Q" in the first box. Then a student responds. The observer marks a "T" (for "tells/makes a comment") in the box diagonally across from the teacher box. If a second student asks a question, a "Q" is recorded in the next box. Then, the teacher tells or says something and a "T" goes in the box on the teacher line. By the end of the discussion, you have a clear pattern of student and teacher interaction. An example is provided on page 134.

EVALUATION FORM:

TEACHER AND STUDENT INTERACTIONS

As the discussion proceeds, mark in the following squares each time the teacher asks a question (Q) or tells/makes a comment (T) and each time the students ask a question (Q) or tells/makes a comment. Record in the order that each question or comment occurs. Count tallies at the end for ratios and totals. Use the information to see how student/teacher interaction is in your classroom.

TEACHER										
STUDENT										

TEACHER	Q		T							
STUDENT		T	Q							

TEACHER										
STUDENT										

TEACHER										
STUDENT										

TEACHER										
STUDENT										

TEACHER										
STUDENT										

TOTALS: TT _____ TQ _____ ST _____ SQ _____

RATIOS: TT _____ TQ _____ ST _____ SQ _____

This form was adapted from the Observation Data Form in the Taba Teaching Strategy manuals. See Institute for Staff Development, eds., *Hilda Taba Teaching Strategies Program*, units 1,2,3,4. Miami, Fla.: Author, 1971.

The teacher will not give opinions or value judgments.

Observation Form #5 can be used for evaluating this teacher strategy. The coach or observer writes down teacher responses to students. The responses are then coded, using the codes on the bottom of the sheet: "O" for teacher opinion, "V" for teacher value judgment, "GRP" for total group response, and "NON" for nonjudgmental response.

The teacher will not repeat student responses.

Observation Form #5 can also be used to code repeating behavior. Responses can also be coded with an "R," teacher repeats student. Also, Observation Form #1, the general scripting form, can be used to detect any repeating behavior.

The teacher will ask students to reflect on their thinking.

Either Observation Form #1 or #2 can be used for this strategy. A general script will show you what type of questions the teacher asks; however, Form #2 will provide you with even more specific data.

In order to use the forms we suggest, you must be familiar with the teacher strategies we describe. Only then can you observe and code. However, if necessary, a peer coach can record the data and the teacher can code later.

Student Behaviors

When evaluating student behaviors, you have a number of options also available to you: (1) you can evaluate the students' behavior; (2) other individuals, such as the peer coach, can evaluate the students' behavior; and (3) the student can evaluate his or her own behavior.

Two general forms can be used by either teacher or students—The Student Self-Evaluation Questionnaire, Form A and Form B. The questions on both forms are representative of the nine student behaviors; three questions are given for each student behavior.* Description of their use is given on the form. In essence, the forms can be used in a (1) a pre- or posttest format, (2) for the student's own personal use, or (3) as a discussion starter.

---

*Please note: we created these questions for our own use. They have not been tested for scientific validity or reliability. Feel free to change or add as necessary.

Student Self-Evaluation
QUESTIONNAIRE

FORMS

Be aware that these forms address only the student behaviors that may occur in a classroom discussion format. If a student has difficulty speaking in class, it must not be interpreted that he or she isn't thinking. This form is designed to measure overt behavior.

Form A (page 137) has alternately positive and negative statements about thinking behaviors. Students could use this evaluation to total up all the scores for the even-numbered questions and all the scores for the odd-numbered questions and compare. This form is best used for group discussions, as some of the items may be expanded upon by the students.

Form B (page 138) is correlated to the nine student behaviors. There are three items per behavior. Use this survey as a pre- and post-test. Look for an increase in scores over time.

HOW TO USE

The student self-evaluation is designed for the student to think about his or her behavior/attitude in a classroom discussion. It can be used in three ways:

1—FOR STUDENTS: It can be used strictly as a springboard for discussion and for the students' eyes only. The students could be involved in the pre/post format by allowing them to score the last test. The first test could then be returned. They could compare and discuss (or write about the changes in their attitudes/ behaviors).

2—FOR TEACHER: It can be used as a pre- and posttest instrument for the teacher (Form B is better for this).

3—FOR PARENTS: The change in the scores, along with the tally sheet, could be shared at parent-teacher conferences in the context of evaluating participation (some report cards require grades for "Speaking" and "Listening").

COMPARE WITH TALLY SHEETS

The student self-evaluation can be compared with the tally sheets to see if the student attitudes and actual behaviors correlate.

A

STUDENT SELF-EVALUATION

Picture yourself in a classroom. Rate the statements below about yourself. 1=NEVER, 2=SELDOM, 3=SOMETIMES, and 4=ALWAYS. Circle the number that best describes yourself in each situation.

	NEVER	SEL-DOM	SOME-TIMES	AL-WAYS
1. In a class discussion I'm always anxious to talk.	1	2	3	4
2. I feel embarrassed to raise my hand.	1	2	3	4
3. Sometimes I think I know things before other people.	1	2	3	4
4. I worry that I can't remember things.	1	2	3	4
5. I enjoy trying to get people to agree with me.	1	2	3	4
6. I feel bored in class discussions.	1	2	3	4
7. I don't like waiting to be called upon.	1	2	3	4
8. When other kids talk I worry I'll forget what they are saying.	1	2	3	4
9. I like to talk about controversial topics.	1	2	3	4
10. I usually hope the teacher won't notice me.	1	2	3	4
11. I think my ideas are very different from other people's.	1	2	3	4
12. I feel uncomfortable in class discussions.	1	2	3	4
13. I like to discuss things with my parents or friends.	1	2	3	4
14. I worry that the other kids will laugh at what I say.	1	2	3	4
15. I enjoy listening to everyone's ideas, then talking.	1	2	3	4
16. Everybody's ideas seem better than mine.	1	2	3	4
17. I enjoy the topics teachers choose for discussion.	1	2	3	4
18. I worry that I'm not smart enough to discuss things in class.	1	2	3	4
19. I enjoy long discussions.	1	2	3	4
20. I'm afraid to talk in a group.	1	2	3	4
21. I like discussing books I've read.	1	2	3	4
22. I avoid discussions at home about school.	1	2	3	4
23. I enjoy writing about things the class has discussed.	1	2	3	4
24. I feel more comfortable writing answers than discussing them.	1	2	3	4
25. I can disagree with someone without getting mad.	1	2	3	4
26. I prefer not to talk in class discussions.	1	2	3	4
27. I like to get other people to agree with what I think.	1	2	3	4
28. I'm very nervous when I think I'm going to be called upon.	1	2	3	4
29. I like to hear what other people think.	1	2	3	4
30. I like to think about things.	1	2	3	4

B
STUDENT SELF-EVALUATION

Picture yourself in a classroom. Rate the statements below about yourself. 1=NEVER, 2=SELDOM, 3=SOMETIMES, and 4=ALWAYS. Circle the number that best describes yourself in each situation.

	NEVER	SEL-DOM	SOME-TIMES	AL-WAYS
1. I enjoy listening to everyone's ideas in my class.	1	2	3	4
2. I listen to others first, then give my ideas after I think.	1	2	3	4
3. I believe there's usually more than one way to figure out a problem.	1	2	3	4
4. I can think about things for a long while without getting bored.	1	2	3	4
5. I have to know why something is true.	1	2	3	4
6. When I am explaining something in class, I find words to use that best tell what I want to say.	1	2	3	4
7. I like to talk about controversial topics.	1	2	3	4
8. I ask questions that make other people think.	1	2	3	4
9. I can explain to my friends how I figured out a problem.	1	2	3	4
10. I enjoy long discussions.	1	2	3	4
11. I choose my words carefully so others can understand.	1	2	3	4
12. I try to figure out why I believe certain things.	1	2	3	4
13. In class, I am always eager to talk.	1	2	3	4
14. When I'm trying to figure out something, I can picture it in my head.	1	2	3	4
15. I try to think up hard questions to try to answer.	1	2	3	4
16. When kids talk in class, I remember what they say.	1	2	3	4
17. Different ideas occur to me when I think about a problem.	1	2	3	4
18. I don't give up on problems easily.	1	2	3	4
19. I think first before I give my ideas.	1	2	3	4
20. I can describe an idea using just a few words.	1	2	3	4
21. I can think of reasons for why I believe something.	1	2	3	4
22. If I don't understand a problem right away, I stick with it till I do.	1	2	3	4
23. Class discussions are one of my favorite activities.	1	2	3	4
24. I like trying to figure out a difficult problem, even if I have to think about it for a long time.	1	2	3	4
25. When I hear about something new, questions occur to me that I want to ask.	1	2	3	4
26. I can usually give more than one answer to the question.	1	2	3	4
27. I talk to myself in my head.	1	2	3	4

The second and third general forms we have developed are the "Student Self-Evaluation—Lesson" and the "Student Self-Evaluation—Unit" forms. These forms asks students to reflect on their performance during the thinking lesson. Students can fill out the forms after the lesson; the teacher can decide whether the students share the forms with him or her. The cutoff at the bottom allows feedback for the teacher without revealing the student's name. In chapter 7, we also provided students with evaluation sheets for their own use. Have students keep these in a thinking notebook or start a thinking journal.

Let's look at ideas for evaluating specific student behaviors.

The student will participate.

Participation by students can be evaluated using Student Response Form #1 in appendix C. A description of how this can be used is given on the form. Students can act as recorders, as we mentioned in chapter 7 (see page 103).

The student will give reasons for answers. The student will use precise, specific words. The student will offer different answers to one problem. The student will ask complex-thinking questions about the topic.

These four behaviors all use similar forms. As we were developing the forms, we realized that they evaluate content, thinking processes, and student behaviors simultaneously. You will see that the forms we suggest can give you a wealth of information concerning student thinking. In addition, by using a set form, you or your students can keep a record of events in the thoughtful classroom.

Student Response Form #2 can be used for reasoning behaviors. As you can see from the directions, student responses can be evaluated for depth of reasoning as well as number of thoughts.

The student will take time to think about the problem and will be comfortable with the amount of time a discussion takes. The student will stick with a problem, even though it might be difficult.

These two behaviors are more difficult to assess because of the difficulty in defining them by specific actions. The first behavior focuses on group interaction; the second behavior concerns the student's personal interaction with a problem. Either behavior could be evaluated using the general student evaluation forms we mentioned earlier.

STUDENT SELF-EVALUATION—*Lesson*

Check the behavior you chose to work on:

☐ Participating   ☐ Offering different answers to one problem

☐ Giving reasons for answers   ☐ Listening to what other students are saying

☐ Using precise and specific words   ☐ Thinking about my thinking

☐ Taking time to think about the problem   ☐ Asking complex questions about the topic

☐ Sticking to the problem

How many times do you think you showed the behavior?

_____
_____
_____
_____
_____

What will you do differently in the next thinking lesson?

_____
_____
_____
_____

Show that this topic held your attention. Write two major new ideas you learned.

_____
_____
_____
_____
_____

- ✂ -

NOTE TO THE TEACHER:

	Do not Agree			Strongly Agree
1. At the beginning of the lesson you made me understand how I was supposed to think.	1	2	3	4
2. I really had to think during today's lesson.	1	2	3	4
3. I feel that I got an equal opportunity to express my ideas.	1	2	3	4
4. Sometimes it is hard for me to understand you.	1	2	3	4

5. Next time it would help me learn better if you

_____
_____
_____
_____
_____
_____

STUDENT SELF-EVALUATION—*Unit*

Look back over our study of _____
Think about how you did. Answer these questions:

List the thinking behaviors you used.

_____
_____
_____
_____

Give three major new ideas you learned.

_____
_____
_____
_____

Tell how your thinking about the topic changed.

_____
_____
_____
_____

What would you still like to know about the topic?

_____
_____
_____
_____

- ✂ -

NOTE TO THE TEACHER:

	Do not Agree			Strongly Agree
1. You always made me understand what I was to do.				
2. I really had to think during lessons.	1	2	3	4
3. I feel that I got an equal opportunity to express my ideas.	1	2	3	4
4. Sometimes it is hard for me to understand you.	1	2	3	4
	1	2	3	4

5. I would suggest the following changes to the unit:

_____
_____
_____
_____
_____
_____

In addition, we have found it to be useful to videotape a thinking activity or discussion and then show the tapes to students. Ask students to evaluate their comfort level with the discussion and their ability to stick with a problem. Students enjoy watching themselves on videotape and will be able to observe behaviors.

The student will listen to what other students say.

This behavior can be evaluated using the Teacher Observation Form #1. After the lesson is scripted, the observer goes back and codes student responses to each other. We make the assumption that you have taught students the appropriate ways of acknowledging other students that we mentioned in chapter 7.

The student will think about his or her thinking.

This behavior is a difficult one to evaluate. In fact, we have had little success in developing any type of measurable, standard process to use when assessing student metacognition. However, we have two suggestions.

First, students can be asked to write about their thinking process. Student thinking logs or journals can be kept and then evaluated regularly by the teacher, much the same way holistic writing samples are graded. The teacher can look for key phrases or descriptions that would indicate self-awareness of thinking. The journals could be open-ended, or students could be given a leading question or statement to respond to such as "describe the steps you used to solve the problem." Another idea is to have students describe orally their thinking, with open-ended or directed questions.

Using either technique has one inevitable drawback. The good thinkers in your classroom who lack oral, written, or vocabulary skills are at a disadvantage. Poor writing or oral skills can overshadow the evaluation and lead to a misunderstanding of a student's thinking ability.

The following table sums up the different evaluation forms we have discussed in this chapter.

Summary of
EVALUATION FORMS

TEACHER STRATEGIES

OBSERVATION FORM #1

Scripting entire lesson for:
The teacher will focus and refocus students on the task.
The teacher will ask extension questions.
The teacher will accept a variety of student responses.
The teacher will not repeat student responses.

OBSERVATION FORM #2:

The teacher will focus and refocus students on the task.
The teacher will ask open-ended questions.
The teacher will ask extension questions.

OBSERVATION FORM #3:

The teacher will wait for student responses.

OBSERVATION FORM #4a (scripting form):

The teacher will accept a variety of student responses.

OBSERVATION FORM #4b (tally form):

The teacher will accept a variety of student responses.

OBSERVATION FORM #5:

The teacher will not give opinions or value judgments.
The teacher will not repeat student responses.

STUDENT BEHAVIORS

Student Self-Evaluation Questionnaire (A)
Student Self-Evaluation Questionnaire (B)
Student Self-Evaluation—Lesson
Student Self-Evaluation—Unit
Student Response Form #1

The student will participate.
Voluntary participation
Involuntary participation
The student will listen to others.
The student will give reasons for answers.

Student Response Form #2

The student will give reasons for answers.

Student Response Form #3
The student will use precise, specific words.

Student Response Form #4
The student will offer different answers to one problem.

Student Response Form #5
The student will ask complex-thinking questions about the topic.

Conclusion

Evaluation is a challenging undertaking and yet, without it, you cannot create the thoughtful classroom. In this chapter, we have discussed a number of different ways to evaluate the thinking of your students and your teaching: standardized tests of thinking and classroom climate, teacher-made assessments, and myriad observation forms.

Given the amount of information, the task of evaluating the teaching of thinking may seem overwhelming as you read this chapter. Don't be dismayed or discouraged. Our purpose was to present you with options. You probably will not use all the ideas or materials suggested here. We assume that you are a tour guide with a mind of your own. Look at our ideas; take what you need and leave the rest. Design your own forms if none of ours work. Whether you use our ideas or others, learn from your successes and failures. Only then can you truly say you have a thoughtful classroom.

Notes

Chapter 1

1. See, for example, the following two reports: National Commission on Excellence in Education, U.S. Department of Education, *A Nation at Risk: The Imperative for Educational Reform* (Washington, D.C., 1983); and National Science Foundation, *Educating Americans for the 21st Century* (Washington, D.C., 1983).

2. See, for example, the recent survey conducted by The National Alliance of Businesses, reported in "Businesses Aren't Satisfied with New Workers, Poll Finds," *Arizona Daily Star*, 16 July 1990.

3. F. Newman and M. Lipman, "Which Aspects of Teaching Thinking Are Distinctive to Particular Subjects?" presentation at the Association for Supervision and Curriculum Development, National Curriculum Study Institute: Teaching Complex Thinking in School Subjects, Alexandria, Va., December 1989.

Chapter 2

1. See "Restructuring: What Is It?" *Educational Leadership* 47, no. 7 (1990).

2. L. Resnick, "What Does Research Suggest about Transfer of Intellectual Skills?" presentation at the Association for Supervision and Curriculum Development, National Curriculum Study Institute: Teaching Complex Thinking in School Subjects, Alexandria, Va., December 1989.

3. See "Preparing Today's Students for Tomorrow's World," *Educational Leadership* 47, no. 1 (1989).

4. See R. H. Ennis, "Critical Thinking and Subject Specificity: Clarification and Needed Research," *Educational Researcher* 18 (1989): 4–10.

5. See J. Kruse and B. Presseisen, *A Catalog of Programs for Teaching Thinking* (Philadelphia: Research for Better Schools, 1987); and R. S. Nickerson et al., *The Teaching of Thinking* (Hillsdale, N.J.: Lawrence Erlbaum, 1985).

6. R. J. Swartz, *Structured Thinking for Critical Thinking and Reasoning in Standard Subject Area Instruction* (Unpublished manuscript, 1989).

7. The idea of "selective abandonment" was presented during a large-group discussion at the Association for Supervision and Curriculum Development, National Curriculum Study Institute: Teaching Complex Thinking in School Subjects, Alexandria, Va., December 1989.

Chapter 3

1. A. L. Costa, "Toward a Model of Human Intellectual Functioning," in A. L. Costa, ed., *Developing Minds: A Resource Book for Teaching Thinking* (Alexandria, Va.: Association for Supervision and Curriculum Development, 1985).

2. B. K. Beyer, "Improving Thinking Skills: Defining the Problem," *Phi Delta Kappan* 65 (April 1984): 486.

3. R. Paul, "An Open Letter to Participants in the ASCD Conference on Complex Thinking" (Unpublished communication, 1989).

4. B. K. Beyer, *Developing a Thinking Skills Program* (Boston: Allyn and Bacon, 1988); D. E. Burns, *Methods and Materials for the Direct Teaching of Thinking Skills,* paper presented at the annual National Association for Gifted Children Convention, Orlando, Fla., November 1988; A. L. Costa and B. Presseisen, "Appendix A: A Glossary of Thinking Skills," in A. L. Costa, ed., *Developing Minds: A Resource Book for Teaching Thinking* (Alexandria, Va.: Association for Supervision and Curriculum Development, 1985); R. H. Ennis, "A Taxonomy of Critical Thinking Dispositions and Abilities," in J. B. Baron and R. J. Sternberg, eds., *Teaching Thinking Skills: Theory and Practice* (New York: W. H. Freeman and Co., 1987); and R. J. Sternberg, "Critical Thinking: Its Nature, Measurement, and Improvement," in F. R. Link, ed., *Essays on the Intellect* (Alexandria, Va.: Association for Supervision and Curriculum Development, 1985).

5. P. Torrance, *Encouraging Creativity in the Classroom* (Dubuque, Ia.: William C. Brown Co., 1970).

6. See Burns, *Methods and Materials;* and D. J. Treffinger, *Encouraging Creative Learning for the Gifted and Talented: A Handbook of Methods and Techniques* (Ventura, Calif.: Ventura County Superintendent of Schools, 1980).

7. See D. J. Treffinger, *Encouraging Creative Thinking.*

8. R. J. Marzano et al., *Dimensions of Thinking: A Framework for Curriculum and Instruction* (Alexandria, Va., Association for Supervision and Curriculum Development, 1988), 17.

9. Beyer, Costa, and Presseisen, "Improving Thinking Skills," "Appendix A," and S. J. Parnes, *Programming Creative Behavior* (Buffalo, N.Y.: State University of New York at Buffalo, 1966).

10. Beyer, "Improving Thinking Skills"; and J. Saphier et al., *How to Make Decisions That Stay Made* (Alexandria, Va.: Association for Supervision and Curriculum Development).

11. The difference between problem solving and decision making is described in R. Beyth-Marom et al., *Teaching Decision Making to Adolescents: A Critical Review* (Washington, D.C.: Carnegie Council on Adolescent Development, 1989). (Available from the Carnegie Corporation of New York, 11 Dupont Circle, N.W., Washington, D.C. 20036).

12. A. L. Costa, "The Principal's Role in Enhancing Thinking Skills," in A. L. Costa, ed., *Developing Minds: A Resource Book for Teaching Thinking* (Alexandria, Va.: Association for Supervision and Curriculum Development, 1985).

13. See E. Bondy, "Thinking about Thinking," *Childhood Education* (March/April 1984): 234–38; J. H. Flavell, *Cognitive Development* (Englewood Cliffs, N.J.: Prentice-Hall, 1977); S. G. Paris et al., "Informed Strategies for Learning: A Program to Improve Children's Reading Awareness and Comprehension," *Journal of Educational Psychology* 76 (1984): 1239–52; and A. Whimby, "Students Can Learn to Be Better Problem Solvers," *Educational Leadership* 37, no. 7 (1980): 56–65.

14. A. L. Costa, "Teacher Behaviors That Enable Student Thinking," in A. L. Costa, ed., *Developing Minds: A Resource Book for Teaching Thinking* (Alexandria, Va.: Association for Supervision and Curriculum Development, 1985).

15. See, for example, R. H. Ennis, "Critical Thinking and Subject Specificity: Clarification and Needed Research," *Educational Researcher* 18 (1989): 16–25.

16. D. N. Perkins and G. Salomon, "Are Cognitive Skills Context Bound?" *Educational Researcher* 18 (1989): 16–25.

17. R. S. Nickerson et al., *The Teaching of Thinking* (Hillsdale, N.J.: Lawrence Erlbaum, 1985).

18. R. Baum, "10 Top Programs," *Learning* (February 1990): 51–55.

19. References for these and other thinking programs can be found in the following sources: R. Baum, "10 Top Programs"; P. Chance, *Thinking in the Classroom: A Survey of Programs* (New York: Teachers College Press, 1985); Costa, "Teacher Behaviors"; J. Kruse and B. Z. Presseisen, *A Catalog of Programs for Teaching Thinking* (Philadelphia: Research for Better Schools, 1987); Nickerson et al., *The Teaching of Thinking;* and R. K. Wagner and R. J. Sternberg, "Alternative Conceptions of Intelligence and Their Implications for Education," *Review of Educational Research* 54 (1984): 197–224.

Chapter 4

1. See, for example, J. D. Long and R. L. Williams, *Strategies of Self-improvement for Teachers* (Princeton, N.J.: Princeton Book Company, 1982). Magazines for teachers are good resources—e.g., *Learning* and *Instructor*; R. L. Curwin and A. N. Mendler, *Discipline with Dignity* (Alexandria, Va.: Association for Supervision and Curriculum Development, 1988); R. Dreikus et al., *Maintaining Sanity in the Classroom: Classroom Management Techniques*, 2d ed. (New York: Harper and Row, 1982); *Other Side of the Report Card: A How-to-Do-It Program for Affective Education* (Santa Monica, Calif.: Goodyear Publishing Co.); and W. J. Kreidler, *Creative Conflict Resolution: More Than 200 Activities for Keeping Peace in the Classroom* (Glenview, Ill.: Scott, Foresman and Co., 1984).

2. R. J. Swartz and D. N. Perkins, *Teaching Thinking: Issues and Approaches* (Pacific Grove, Calif.: Midwest Publications, 1989).

3. R. S. Nickerson, "Kinds of Thinking Taught in Current Programs," *Educational Leadership* 42, no. 1 (1984): 34.

Chapter 5

1. One resource with great ideas similar to the ones we have listed is S. H. Hawley and R. C. Hawley, *A Teacher's Handbook of Practical Strategies for Teaching Thinking in the Classroom* (Amherst, Mass.: ERA Press, 1987).

2. A number of books are also available with similar information and ideas on how to restructure current curriculum with sample lessons. See, for example, L. B. Resnick and L. E. Klopfer, eds., *Toward the Thinking Curriculum: Current Cognitive Research* (Alexandria, Va.: Association for Supervision and Curriculum Development, 1989). This book lists some detailed lessons, and although they are not identified as restructured, they are in fact that. See also B. F. Jones et al., *Strategic Teaching and Learning: Cognitive Instruction in the Content Areas* (Alexandria, Va.: Association for Supervision and Curriculum Development, 1987). This gives sample lessons in the four main disciplines. Sample lessons can be found in M. Heiman and J. Slomianko, eds., *Thinking Skills Instruction: Concepts and Techniques* (Washington, D.C.: National Education Association, 1987); R. Paul et al., *Critical Thinking Handbook: 4th–6th Grades. A Guide for Remodeling Lesson Plans in Language Arts, Social Studies, and Science* (Rohnert Park, Calif.: Center for Critical Thinking and Moral Critique, Sonoma State University, 1987). (The center has remodeling books for other grade levels as well. Write to the center for a comprehensive bibliography of other materials for sale: Center for Critical Thinking and Moral Critique, Sonoma State University, Rohnert Park, CA 94928.)

3. Resources for teaching thinking in social studies include D. Alvermann, "Strategic Teaching in Social Studies," in B. F. Jones et al., eds., *Strategic Teaching and Learning: Cognitive Instruction in the Content Areas* (Alexandria, Va.: Association for Supervision and Curriculum Development, 1987); A. A. Hyde and M. Bizar, *Thinking in context: Teaching Cognitive Processes Across the Elementary School Curriculum* (White Plains, N.Y.: Longman, Inc., 1989); F. M. Newmann, "Higher Order Thinking in the Teaching of Social Studies: Connections Between Theory and Practice," in D. Perkins et al., eds., *Informal Reasoning and Education* (Hillsdale, N.J.: L. Erlbaum, in press); and E. Self, *Teaching Significant Social Studies in the Elementary School* (New York: Rand McNally, 1977).

4. Some science materials that are useful for teaching complex-level thinking to elementary and junior-high students include the ESS materials, TOPS, and Descubrimiento. ESS materials and catalogue can be obtained from Delta Education, Inc., P. O. Box M, Nashua, NH 03061-6012. TOPS materials and catalogue can be obtained from Tops Learning Systems, 10970 S. Mulino Rd., Canby, OR 97013. Descubrimiento materials and catalogue can be obtained from Linguametrics Group, P. O. Box 3495, San Rafael, CA 94901.

5. Of course, there are exceptions to this statement. Some published materials do a wonderful job of suggesting complex-level activities and problems. We have listed a number of these in appendix A.

6. We are deeply grateful to Roger Shanley for all his help in developing this lesson.

7. These questions were developed jointly by Shirley Schiever and Anne Udall for a workshop on developing units for publication given in June 1990 at Zephyr Press.

8. E. J. S. Doherty and L. C. Evans, *How to Develop Your Own Curriculum Units* (East Windsor Hill, Conn.: Synergetics, 1984).

9. The best single source for simulation games is Interact, P. O. Box 997, Lakeside, CA 92040.

10. See B. K. Beyer, *Developing a Thinking Skills Program* (Boston: Allyn and Bacon, 1988); and S. Schiever, *A Comprehensive Approach to Teaching Thinking* (Boston: Allyn and Bacon, 1991).

Chapter 6

1. For research to support the use of these behaviors see W. W. Wilen, ed., *Questions, Questioning Techniques, and Effective Teaching* (Washington, D.C.: National Education Association, 1987).

2. T. Levin and R. Long, *Effective Instruction* (Alexandria, Va.: Association for Supervision and Curriculum Development, 1981).

3. *An Introduction to Shared Inquiry* (Chicago: Great Books Foundation, 1987).

4. E. W. Eisner, *The Educational Imagination: On the Design and Evaluation of School Programs* (New York: Macmillan, 1979).

5. A cognitive map is similar to the techniques of webbing or clustering.

6. Two sources support this statement: R. S. Dunn and K. J. Dunn, "Learning Styles/Teaching Styles: Should They. . . Can They. . . Be Matched?" *Educational Leadership* 36 (January 1979): 238–44; and a presentation by Robert Garmston at the annual Association for Supervision and Curriculum Development conference in March 1989.

7. J. T. Dillon, *Teaching and the Art of Questioning* (Bloomington, Ind.: Phi Delta Kappa Educational Foundation, 1983).

8. *Hilda Taba Teaching Strategies Program: Units 1,2,3,4* (Miami, Fla.: Institute for Staff Development, 1971).

9. R. Paul et al., *Critical Thinking Handbook: 4th-6th Grades. A Guide for Remodeling Lesson Plans in Language Arts, Social Studies, and Science* (Rohnert Park, Calif.: Center for Critical Thinking and Moral Critique, Sonoma State University, 1987).

10. There are a number of wonderful resources on questioning strategies and behaviors. The Wilen book (see n.1 above) is a good place to start. Other resources include M. N. Brown and S. M. Keeley, *Asking the Right Questions: A Guide to Critical Thinking* (Englewood Cliffs, N.J.: Prentice-Hall, 1986); C. Cornbleth, *Using Questions in Social Studies* (Arlington, Va.: National Council for the Social Studies, 1977); J. T. Dillon, *Questioning and Teaching: A Manual of Practice* (New York: Teachers College Press, 1988); *Hilda Taba Teaching Strategies Program: Units 1,2,3,4* (Miami, Fla.: Institute for Staff Development, 1971); and S. Schiever, *A Comprehensive Approach to Teaching Thinking* (Boston: Allyn and Bacon, 1991).

11. M. B. Rowe, "Using Wait Time to Stimulate Inquiry," in W. W. Wilen, ed., *Questions, Questioning Techniques, and Effective Teaching* (Washington, D.C.: National Education Association, 1987).

12. Ibid.

13. Ibid.

14. Cooperative learning materials are easy to find in any educational catalogue. Good places to start include N. Graves and T. Graves, *What Is Cooperative Learning: Tips for Teachers 'n' Trainers* (Santa Cruz, Calif.: Cooperative College of California, 1988); D. W. Johnson et al., *Circles of Learning: Cooperation in the Classroom*, rev. ed. (Edina, Minn.: Interaction Book Co., 1986); and D. W. Johnson and R. Johnson, *Learning Together and Alone: Cooperative, Competitive, and Individualistic Learning*, 2d ed. (Englewood Cliffs, N.J.: Prentice-Hall, 1987). Also, write Cooperative College of California for a catalogue full of useful materials: Cooperative College of California, 136 Liberty St., Santa Cruz, CA 95060.

15. This idea was given to us by Daphne McKelvey, one of the teachers in the Creating the Thoughtful Classroom project.

16. See B. Auvine et al., *A Manual for Group Facilitators* (Madison, Wis.: Center for Conflict Resolution, 1978); J. H. Bushman and S. K. Jones, *Effective Communication: A Handbook of Discussion Skills* (Buffalo, N.Y.: DOK Publishers, 1977); N. Drew, *Learning the Skills of Peacemaking: An Activity Guide for Elementary Age Children on Communicating, Cooperating and Resolving Conflict* (Jalmar Press, Rolling Hills Estates, Calif., 1987); D. W. Johnson and F. Johnson, *Joining*

Together: Group Theory and Group Skills (Englewood Cliffs, N.J.: Prentice-Hall, 1987); D. Pincus, *Interactions: More Effective Communication among Parents, Students and Teachers* (Carthage, Ill.: Good Apple, 1988); G. Stanford, *Developing Effective Classroom Groups: A Practical Guide for Teachers* (New York: Hart Publishing Co., 1977); and G. Stanford and B. D. Stanford, *Learning Discussion Skills Through Games* (Englewood Cliffs, N.J.: Citation Press, 1969).

17. A. L. Costa, "Teaching for Intelligent Behavior," presentation at the annual Arizona Association for the Gifted and Talented, Phoenix, Arizona, October 1987.

18. M. D. Gall and T. Rhody, "Review of Research on Questioning Techniques," in W. W. Wilen, ed., *Questions, Questioning Techniques, and Effective Teaching* (Washington, D.C.: National Education Association, 1987).

19. See, for example, the readings in A. L. Costa, ed., *Developing Minds: A Resource Book for Teaching Thinking* (Alexandria, Va.: Association for Supervision and Curriculum Development, 1985).

20. Other sources with ideas on how to teach metacognitive techniques include E. Bondy, "Thinking about Thinking: Encouraging Children's Use of Metacognitive Processes," *Childhood Education* (March/April 1984): 234–38; A. L. Costa, "Mediating the Metacognitive," *Educational Leadership* 42 (November 1984): 57–62; A. L. Costa, ed., *Developing Minds: A Resource Book for Teaching Thinking* (Alexandria, Va.: Association for Supervision and Curriculum Development, 1985); S. H. Hawley and R. C. Hawley, *A Teacher's Handbook of Practical Strategies for Teaching Thinking in the Classroom* (Amherst, Mass.: ERA Press, 1987); L. L. Meeks, "Developing Metacognition in Composition with Peer Response Groups," in M. Heiman and J. Slomianko, eds., *Thinking Skills Instruction: Concepts and Techniques* (Washington, D.C.: National Educational Association, 1987); I. M. Tiedt et al., *Teaching Thinking in K-12 Classrooms: Ideas, Activities, and Resources* (Boston: Allyn and Bacon, 1989); and A. Whimby, "Students Can Learn to Be Better Problem Solvers," *Educational Leadership* 37 (April 1980): 560–65.

21. One book about the brain written for elementary students would be a good place to start: S. Gilbert, *Using Your Head: The Many Ways of Being Smart* (New York: Macmillan, 1984).

22. See S. C. Bartoletti and E. S. Lisandrelli, *Study Skills Workout* (Glenview, Ill.: Good Year Books, 1987); L. Colligan, *Scholastic's A+ Guide to Research and Term Papers* (New York: Scholastic, Inc., 1981); D. B. Ellis, *Becoming a Master Student* (Rapid City, S.D.: College Survival, Inc., 1985); E. P. Jensen, *Superteaching* (Del Mar, Calif.: Turning Point, 1988); S. Schiever and R. Shanley, *Mind Over Matter: Life Organization Guide* (Tucson, Ariz.: Zephyr Press, in press); and R. F. Wagner, *Study Skills for Better Grades* (Portland, Me.: J. Weston Walch, 1978).

23. A list of problem-solving strategies can be found in J. McTighe and F. T. Lyman, Jr., "Cueing Thinking in the Classroom: The Promise of Theory-embedded Tools," *Educational Leadership* 45 (April 1988): 18–24.

Chapter 7

1. See notes 13 and 14 in chapter 6 for excellent resources on cooperative learning and group discussion. Appendix A also includes useful material in this area.

2. B. F. Jones et al., "Teaching Students to Construct Graphic Representations," *Educational Leadership* (December 1988/January 1989): 20–25; N. Margulies, *Mapping Inner Space: Learning and Teaching Mind Mapping* (Tucson, Ariz.: Zephyr Press, 1991); and J. McTighe and F. T. Lyman, Jr., "Cueing Thinking in the Classroom: The Promise of Theory-embedded Tools," *Educational Leadership* 45 (April 1988): 18–24.

3. B. F. Jones et al., eds., "Strategic Thinking: A Cognitive Focus," *Strategic Teaching and Learning: Cognitive Instruction in the Content Areas* (Alexandria, Va.: Association for Supervision and Curriculum Development, 1987).

4. See, for example, K. Butler, *It's All in Your Mind: A Student's Guide to Learning Style* (Columbia, Conn.: Learners Dimension, 1988); B. McCarthy, *The Format System: Teaching to Learning Styles with Right-Left Mode Techniques* (Barrington, Ill.: Excel, Inc., 1980); and *Student Learning Styles: Diagnosing and Prescribing Programs* (Reston, Va.: National Association of Secondary School Principals, 1979).

5. See other questions in P. G. O'Daffer and R. I. Charles, "Problem-Solving Tips for Teachers," *Arithmetic Teacher* (January 1988): 26–27.

6. See J. McTighe and F. T. Lyman Jr., "Cueing Thinking in the Classroom: The Promise of Theory-embedded Tools," *Educational Leadership* 45 (April 1988): 19.

7. Good sources for teaching students to become better questioners include S. H. Hawley and R. C. Hawley, *A Teacher's Handbook of Practical Strategies for Teaching Thinking in the Classroom* (Amherst, Mass.: ERA Press, 1987); F. P. Hunkins, "Students as Key Questioners," in W. W. Wilen, ed., *Questions, Questioning Techniques, and Effective Teaching* (Washington, D.C.: National Education Association, 1987); C. W. Lindsey, *Teaching Students to Teach Themselves* (New York: Nichols Publishing, 1988); and J. T. Dillon, *The Practice of Questioning* (New York: Routledge, 1990).

Chapter 8

1. Definition is taken from *The American Heritage Dictionary*, 1972.

2. Other lists of thinking tests are available in J. A. Arter and J. R. Salmon, *A Consumer's Guide: Assessing Higher-Order Thinking Skills* (Portland, Ore.: Northwest Regional Educational Laboratory, 1987); R. H. Ennis "Resource B: Tests That Could Be Called Critical Thinking Tests," in A. L. Costa, ed., *Developing Minds: A Resource Book for Teaching Thinking* (Alexandria, Va.: Association for Supervision and Curriculum Development, 1985).

3. G. Watson and E. M. Glaser, *The Watson-Glaser Critical Thinking Appraisal* (New York: Harcourt, Brace, Jovanovich, 1980).

4. R. H. Ennis and J. Millman, *The Cornell Critical Thinking Test* (Urbana, Ill.: Critical Thinking Project, 1971).

5. V. Shipman, *New Jersey Test of Reasoning Skills, Form B* (Upper Montclair, N.J.: Montclair State College, 1983).

6. *The SEA Test: A Measure of Thinking Skills for the Evaluation of Programs for the Gifted.* Available from the Bureau of Education Research, 264 Ruffner Hall, University of Virginia, Charlottesville, VA 22903.

7. S. Wassermann, "Reflections on Measuring Thinking, While Listening to Mozart's 'Jupiter' Symphony," *Phi Delta Kappan* (January 1989): 365–70.

8. Robert Sternberg highlights some of these issues in "Critical Thinking: Its Nature, Measurement, and Improvement," in F. R. Link, ed., *Essays on the Intellect* (Alexandria, Va.: Association for Supervision and Curriculum Development, 1985).

9. J. M. Steele, *Class Activities Questionnaire* (Mansfield Center, Conn.: Creative Learning Press, 1981).

10. R. J. Stiggins et al., *Measuring Thinking Skills in the Classroom*, rev. ed. (Washington, D.C.: National Education Association, 1988).

11. R. J. Stiggins et al., "Methods and Materials for the Direct Teaching of Thinking Skills," paper presented at the annual National Association for Gifted Children convention, Orlando, Florida, November 1988.

12. R. Garmston, "Cognitive Coaching and Professors' Instructional Thought," *Human Intelligence Newsletter* 10 (1989): 3–4.

13. There are other types of peer coaching in which the coach acts as a mentor and therefore gives advice and counsel. This type of peer coaching can be effective, too, if both partners agree to the mentor relationship. See the February 1987 issue of *Educational Leadership* for a good introduction to peer coaching. Also see P. Raney and P. Robbins, "Professional Growth through Peer Coaching," *Educational Leadership* (May 1989): 35–38. ASCD also has an excellent videotape about peer coaching: "Opening Doors." Videotapes about peer coaching are also available from Kay Hachten Educational Videotapes, P. O. Box 26724, Santa Ana, CA 92799.

14. W. W. Wilen, "Improving Teachers' Questions and Questioning: Research Informs Practice," in W. W. Wilen, ed., *Questions, Questioning Techniques, and Effective Teaching* (Washington, D.C.: National Education Association, 1987).

15. *An Introduction to Shared Inquiry* (Chicago: Great Books Foundation, 1987); and *Hilda Taba Teaching Strategies Program: Units 1,2,3,4.* (Miami, Fla.: Institute for Staff Development, 1971).

Appendix A: Valuable Resources

We consider the following resources invaluable if you are going to teach thinking in your classroom:

Beyer, B. K. "Improving Thinking Skills: Defining the Problem." *Phi Delta Kappan* 65 (1984): 486–90.

Beyer, B. K. "Improving Thinking Skills—Practical Approaches." *Phi Delta Kappan* 65 (1984): 556–60.

Beyer, B. K. *Practical Strategies for the Teaching of Thinking.* Boston: Allyn and Bacon, 1987.

Beyer, B. K. *Developing a Thinking Skills Program.* Boston: Allyn and Bacon, 1988.

Chance, P. *Thinking in the Classroom: A Survey of Programs.* New York: Teachers College Press, 1986.

Costa, A. L., ed. *Developing Minds: A Resource Book for Teaching Thinking.* Alexandria, Va.: Association for Supervision and Curriculum Development, 1985.

Costa, A. L., and L. F. Lowery. *Techniques for Teaching Thinking.* Pacific Grove, Calif.: Midwest Publications, 1989.

Hawley, S. H., and R. C. Hawley. *A Teacher's Handbook of Practical Strategies for Teaching Thinking in the Classroom.* Amherst, Mass.: ERA Press, 1987.

Heiman, M., and J. Slomianko, eds. *Thinking Skills Instruction: Concepts and Techniques.* Washington, D.C.: National Education Association, 1987.

Jones, B. F., et al., eds. *Strategic Teaching and Learning: Cognitive Instruction in the Content Areas.* Alexandria, Va.: Association for Supervision and Curriculum Development, 1987.

Kruse, J., and B. Z. Presseisen. *A Catalog of Programs for Teaching Thinking.* Philadelphia: RBS, 1987.

Marzano, R. J., et al. *Dimensions of Thinking: A Framework for Curriculum and Instruction.* Alexandria, Va.: Association for Supervision and Curriculum Development, 1988.

Nickerson, R. S., et al. *The Teaching of Thinking.* Hillsdale, N.J.: Erlbaum Associates, 1985.

Norris, S. P., and R. H. Ennis. *Evaluating Critical Thinking.* Pacific Grove, Calif.: Midwest Publications, 1989.

Paul, R., et al. *Critical Thinking Handbook: 4th -6th Grades. A Guide for Remodeling Lesson Plans in Language Arts, Social Studies, and Science.* Rohnert Park, Calif.: Center for Critical Thinking and Moral Critique, Sonoma State University, 1987.

Perkins, D. N. *Knowledge as Design.* Hillsdale, N.J.: Erlbaum Associates, 1986.

Presseisen, B. Z. *Thinking Skills: Research and Practice.* Washington, D.C.: National Education Association, 1986.

Raths, L. E., et al. *Teaching for Thinking: Theory and Application.* Columbus, Ohio: Charles E. Merrill, 1967.

Resnick, L. B., and L. E. Klopfer, eds. *Toward the Thinking Curriculum: Current Cognitive Research.* Alexandria, Va.: Association for Supervision and Curriculum Development, 1989.

Schiever, S. *A Comprehensive Approach to Teaching Thinking.* Boston: Allyn and Bacon, 1991.

Swartz, R. J., and D. N. Perkins. *Teaching Thinking: Issues and Approaches.* Pacific Grove, Calif.: Midwest Publications, 1989.

Tiedt, I. M., et al. *Teaching Thinking in K-12 Classrooms: Ideas, Activities, and Resources.* Boston: Allyn and Bacon, 1989.

Wilen, W. W. *Questioning Skills for Teachers,* 2d ed. Washington, D.C.: National Education Association, 1987.

Wilen, W. W., ed. *Questions, Questioning Techniques, and Effective Teaching.* Washington, D.C.: National Education Association, 1987.

Worsham, A., and A. Stockton. *A Model for Teaching Thinking Skills: The Inclusion Process.* Bloomington, Ind.: Phi Delta Kappa, 1986.

Appendix B:
Types of Questions Used in the Socratic Method

Questions of Clarification

What do you mean by _____?

What is your main point? Could you give me an example? Could you explain that further?

Would you say more about that? What do you think is the main issue here?

Let me see if I understand you, do you mean _____ or _____?

Is your basic point _____ or _____?

What do you think John meant by his remark?

Jane, would you summarize in your own words what Richard has said? Richard, is that what you meant?

How does _____ relate to _____?

Could you put that another way?

Questions that Probe Assumptions

You seem to be assuming _____.
Do I understand you correctly?

All of your reasoning is dependent on the idea that _____.

Why have you based your reasoning on _____ rather than _____?

You seem to be assuming _____.

How would you justify taking this for granted? Is it always the case?

What is Karen assuming? What could we assume instead?

Questions that Probe Reasons and Evidence

How do you know? Why did you say that?

What would be an example? How could we go about finding out whether that is true?

What other information do we need to know?

By what reasoning did you come to that conclusion?

Could you explain your reasons to us?

But is that good evidence to believe?

What are your reasons for saying that? Why do you think that is true?

Do you have any evidence for that? Are those reasons adequate? Is there reason to doubt that evidence?

Who is in a position to know if that is the case? What difference does that make? What would convince you?

Can someone else give evidence to support that response? How does that apply to this case?

Questions about Viewpoints or Perspectives

You seem to be approaching this issue from _____ _____ perspective.

Why have you chosen this rather than _____ _____ perspective?

How would other groups/types of people respond? Why? What would influence them?

How could you answer the objection that _____ _____ would make?

Can/did anyone see this another way?

What would someone who disagrees say?

What is an alternative?

How are Ken's and Roxanne's ideas alike? Different?

Questions that Probe Implications and Consequences

What are you implying by that?

When you say _____ are you implying _____?

But if that happened, what else would also happen as a result?

Why? What effect would that have?

Would that necessarily happen or only probably happen? What is an alternative?

If this and this are the case, then what else must also be true?

Questions about the Question

I'm not sure I understand how you are interpreting the main question at issue.

How can we find out? How could someone settle this question?

To answer this question, what questions would we have to answer first?

Is the question clear? Do we understand it?

Is this the same issue as _____?

Can we break this question down at all?

Do we all agree that this is the question?

Would _____ put the question differently?

How would _____ put the question?

Why is this question important? Is this question easy or hard to answer? Why?

Does this question ask us to evaluate something?

What does this question assume?

This is reprinted with permission from R. Paul, A. J. A. Biner, K. Jensen, and H. Kreklau, *Critical Thinking Handbook: 4th-6th Grades. A Guide for Remodeling Lesson Plans in Language Arts, Social Studies, and Science* (Rohnert Park, Calif.: Center for Critical Thinking and Moral Critique, Sonoma State University, 1987.)

Appendix C: Evaluation Forms

OBSERVATION FORM #1
Scripting

Can be used for the following teacher strategies: The teacher will focus and refocus students on task, the teacher will ask extension questions, the teacher will accept a variety of student responses, and the teacher will not repeat student responses.

Directions: Script everything said for 15 minutes. Use your own abbreviated writing techniques. Look for patterns. Note time every 3 minutes or so in the left column to record a sense of pacing for the lesson.

☐ Tape recording ☐ Videotape ☐ Observer: _____

Date _____ Time beginning: _____ Time ending: _____

Lesson topic: _____

TIME	TEACHER TALK	STUDENT TALK

OBSERVATION FORM #2

The teacher will focus and refocus students, ask open-ended questions, ask extension questions, or ask students for reflective thinking.

Directions: Script only the teacher's questions or requests (questions in the form of a command). After the lesson, code the questions. Look for patterns in the kinds of questions/requests made. Compare with previous observations.

☐ Tape recording   ☐ Videotape   ☐ Observer: _____

Date _____ Time beginning:_____ Time ending: _____

Lesson topic: _____

Question Codes

O *OPEN:* 1–Focusing or refocusing question; 2–Question that asks for reasons; 3–Question that seeks different ideas, a variety of responses; 4–Question that persuades students to clarify; 5–Question that requests rewording for preciseness; 6–Question that requests students to reflect on their thinking.

C *CLOSED:* 1–Question that requires a yes/no answer; 2–Question that requires a fact answer.

I *IRRELEVANT:* Question that is irrelevant to the lesson ("Where is your pencil?" "Why are you late today?" "Did you see the Lakers play?").

TEACHER QUESTIONS/REQUESTS	QUESTION CODE

OBSERVATION FORM #3

The teacher will wait for student responses.

Directions: Write only the questions or requests (questions in the form of commands) given by the teacher. It can be difficult to write questions and count wait time simultaneously. Use a watch with a second hand and note the end of the question, even as you finish writing it down. Compare with previous observations.

☐ Tape recording   ☐ Videotape   ☐ Observer: _____

Date _____ Time beginning: _____ Time ending: _____

Lesson topic: _____

TEACHER QUESTIONS/REQUESTS	WAIT TIME (seconds)

OBSERVATION FORM #4a

The teacher will accept a variety of responses.

Directions: Script the teacher's questions/requests of the lesson. Count the number of student responses to that question (before another is asked). Compare with previous observations.

☐ Tape recording   ☐ Videotape   ☐ Observer: _____

Date _____ Time beginning:_____ Time ending: _____

Lesson topic: _____

TEACHER QUESTIONS/REQUESTS	NUMBER OF RESPONSES

NOTES

_____
_____
_____
_____
_____
_____
_____

TEACHER STRATEGIES

OBSERVATION FORM #4b

The teacher will accept a variety of answers.

Date: _____ Coder's name: _____

Lesson Topic: _____Time beginning:_____ Time ending: _____

Directions: Decide what participation type you will count. A second observer may also tally for another kind of participation. Before beginning, note the students who are absent. The observer may be asked to stop the teacher from calling on the same person a third time. Analyze the results.

PARTICIPATION TYPE: ☐ All Participation   ☐ Hand Raised   ☐ Hand Not Raised

TOTAL	TALLY MARKS	STUDENT NAMES

COMMENTS

_____

_____

_____

_____

_____

_____

OBSERVATION FORM #5

The teacher will not give opinions or value judgments; the teacher will not repeat student responses.

Directions: Script only the teacher's responses after a student speaks. Include "OK," "Uh huh," "Right," and other one-liners. Nonverbal cues may be included parenthetically if the observer has time. Compare to previous observations.

☐ Tape recording   ☐ Videotape   ☐ Observer: _____

Date _____ Time beginning:_____ Time ending: _____

Lesson topic: _____

Coding Responses
O—Teacher OPINION; **V**—Teacher VALUE JUDGMENT; **R**—Teacher REPEATS STUDENT; **GRP**—Total group response ("You were *all* great thinkers!"); **NON**—Nonjudgmental response.

TEACHER RESPONSES	RESPONSE CODE

STUDENT BEHAVIOR: The student will give reasons for answers.
SUGGESTED USES FOR FORM #2

1. Much content lends itself to different views. In social studies almost every war, epoch, and social confrontation has people taking several sides on an issue. Studies of cultures can generate problems such as "If you were told to take one modern thing into the Zulu culture, what would it be and why?" "What was the single most destructive thing the Europeans brought to the Indian culture and why?"

2. In science, experimentation begins with several different hypotheses. Students can state their own hypothesis and give reasons why it is the best choice. Capitalize on those characteristics whenever possible and ask students to take a stand one way or another—with reasons.

3. Most questions you generate will be from the content that you are teaching. However, you may at times want to just evaluate the students' ability to generate reasons on a topic that is familiar to them. You want to emphasize the skill and not the content.

Here are some samples:
- What is the best way to get from school to the mall after dismissal? Why?
- How should tardiness be disciplined? Why?
- Evaluate methods for disposing of styrofoam fast-food containers.
- How should curfew violation be punished? Why?
- Choose a career and prove why it fits you.
- Give reasons for buying a certain make of car.
- Justify eating whale meat.
- Justify allowing 18-year-olds to vote.

STUDENT BEHAVIOR: The student will use precise, specific words.
SUGGESTED USES FOR FORM #3

1. Students can use this sheet to prepare for the discussion to come. It gives "think time." Make sure to use an open-ended question that focuses your students on the content to be studied.

2. This sheet can be used as a summative test of content. For example, "State concisely and precisely what we learned in today's discussion about the rain forests." If the form is used this way, you can tell what major points the student grasped.

3. You can use this sheet to give students practice in expressing themselves concisely. You may want students to practice this behavior on topics that require little background knowledge.

Here are a few examples of problem questions:
- What are the major functions of umpires in sports games?
- Why (or why not) should sports be included in the regular school day?
- What is your opinion about capital punishment for juveniles?
- How does capital punishment help to prevent crime?
- How would legalizing drugs help this country?
- If you were president, how would you word a law to limit the size of U.S. families?
- If you were mayor, how would you word a law to limit the number of pets that a family could have in the city limits?

STUDENT BEHAVIOR:
The student will ask complex-level thinking questions about a topic.
SUGGESTED USES FOR FORM #5

1. Introductory oral exercise for a new topic.

2. Written response could be used before a class discussion, to generate questions, and also give total class "think time."

3. Choose some of the following topics. Assign the written response and follow up with a class discussion that categorizes the questions and organizes the questions for teams to research.

Sample topics: alcohol, funerals, schools, marriage, religion.

STUDENT BEHAVIORS

STUDENT RESPONSE FORM #1

Date: _____ Coder's name: _____

Lesson Topic: _____Time beginning:_____ Time ending: _____

STUDENT BEHAVIOR BEING TALLIED:

☐Voluntary Participation ☐Involuntary Participation ☐Listens to Others ☐Gives Reasons for Answers

STUDENT NAMES	TALLY MARKS	TOTAL

COMMENTS

_____

_____

_____

_____

_____

_____

STUDENT RESPONSE FORM #2

The student will give reasons for answers.

NAME _____ DATE _____

DIRECTIONS: Stated below is a question or problem. You are to answer the question and list as many reasons as you can that helped you decide on your answer. Remember, you are looking for as many different reasons as you can think of. Please number each new reason.

PROBLEM/QUESTION: _____

_____

_____

_____

ANSWER: _____

_____

_____

_____

_____

_____

_____

REASONS: _____

_____

_____

_____

_____

_____

_____

_____

_____

_____

_____

_____

_____

_____

_____

_____

_____

_____

_____

_____

STUDENT RESPONSE FORM #3

The student will use precise, specific words.

NAME _____ DATE _____

DIRECTIONS: A question or problem is stated below. Give your opinion using precise and specific wording. Say all you wish to say but keep it "in a nutshell." Spend as much time thinking as writing. If you wish, use scratch paper to make notes before writing.

PROBLEM/QUESTION: _____

_____

_____

_____

_____

OPINION: _____

_____

_____

_____

_____

_____

_____

_____

_____

_____

_____

_____

_____

_____

_____

COMMENTS

_____

_____

_____

_____

_____

_____

STUDENT RESPONSE FORM #4

The student will offer different answers to one problem.

NAME _____ DATE _____

DIRECTIONS: A problem is stated below. THINK ABOUT THE PROBLEM. Think of different solutions. Write as many solutions as possible.

PROBLEM: _____

_____

_____

_____

Possible answer #1 _____

_____

_____

_____

_____

_____

Possible answer #2 _____

_____

_____

_____

_____

Possible answer #3 _____

_____

_____

_____

_____

Possible answer #4 _____

_____

_____

_____

_____

COMMENTS

_____

_____

_____

_____